Hachette's Illustrated French Primer, Or, The Child's First French Lessons

HACHETTE'S

ILLUSTRATED FRENCH PRIMER

OR THE

Child's First French Lessons.

Works by the same Author.

THE ILLUSTRATED FRENCH PRIMER
Or, the Child's First French Lessons, with numerous illustrations.
1 vol., small 8vo, cloth, price 1s. 6d.

EARLY FRENCH LESSONS.
64 pages, cloth price 8d.

THE FIRST FRENCH BOOK
Grammar, Conversation, and Translation. 208 pages, cloth, price 10d.

THE SECOND FRENCH BOOK
Grammar, Conversation, and Translation. 208 pages, cloth, price 1s.

FIRST STEPS IN FRENCH IDIOMS.
192 pages, cloth, price 1s. 6d.

KEY TO THE FIRST AND SECOND BOOKS AND TO THE FIRST STEPS IN FRENCH IDIOMS.
(For Teachers only). 1 vol., cloth, 2s. 6d.

THE NEW CONVERSATIONAL FIRST FRENCH READER
224 pages, cloth, price 10d.

HACHETTE'S
ILLUSTRATED FRENCH PRIMER

OR THE

CHILD'S FIRST FRENCH LESSONS

Containing the Alphabet, Words, Phrases, and
French Nursery Rhymes.

EDITED BY

HENRI BUÉ, B. ès L.,

FRENCH MASTER AT MERCHANT TAYLORS' SCHOOL, LONDON,
OCCASIONAL EXAMINER H.M.C.S.C.

New Edition.

LIBRAIRIE HACHETTE & Cⁱᵉ
LONDON: 18, KING WILLIAM STREET, CHARING CROSS.
PARIS: 79, BOULEVARD SAINT-GERMAIN.
BOSTON: CARL SCHOENHOF.
1890.
All Rights reserved.

448.
B86

TO

LILIAN HENRIETTE KLEINAU

THIS LITTLE BOOK

Is affectionately inscribed

49955

BY

THE EDITOR.

Dear Mr. Public,

At the sight of this little work dyspeptic people will exclaim, as they always do: " What! another of those books...!" Don't listen to them. Run your eye through the French Primer, and if you think it amusing and instructive buy it for your numerous little boys and girls, thereby delighting

Yours sincerely,

THE EDITOR.

Throughout the book the English is given under the French; but it does not necessarily follow that the English word is the translation of the French word immediately above it.

INTRODUCTION.

INTENDED FOR OUR YOUNG READERS' FRIENDS.

I.—The **French Alphabet** consists of 26 letters:—

A, a, *a*, pronounced like in *ah! bar, far.*
B, b, *b*, ,, ,, *butter.*
C, c, *c*, ,, ,, *certain or cat.**
D, d, *d*, ,, ,, *duck.*
E, e, *e*, ,, ,, *butter.*
F, f, *f*, ,, ,, *fun.*
G, g, *g*, ,, ,, *girl*,† or like *s* in *pleasure*.
H, h, *h*, ,, ,, *herb.*
I, i, *i*, ,, ,, *bill.*
J, j, *j*, ,, like *s* in *pleasure.*
K, k, *k*, ,, ,, *kernel.*
L, l, *l*, ,, ,, *learn.*
M, m, *m*, ,, ,, *menace.*
N, n, *n*, ,, ,, *nerve.*
O, o, *o*, ,, like in English.
P, p, *p*, ,, ,, *perfect.*
Q, q, *q*, ,, ,, *kernel.*
R, r, *r*, ,, ,, *receive.*
S, s, *s*, ,, ,, *search.*
T, t, *t*, ,, ,, *term.*
U, u, *u*, like the German *ü*, but has no corresponding sound in English; something like *u* in *consecutive.*
V, v, *v*, pronounced like in *veneer.*
W, w, *w* (=*dooble v*), only used in words of foreign origin; is sounded like *v*; but it keeps the English pronunciation in words borrowed from the English.
X, x, *x*, pronounced like in *exertion, exercise.*
Y, y, *y*, (*ee greck*) like in *fleet.*
Z, z, *z*, like in English.

* *C* is soft before *e* and *i*, and hard before *a, o, u.*
† *G* is soft before *e* and *i*, and hard before *a, o, u.*

II.—Accents and other signs.

There are *three* accents, placed over the vowels a, e, i, o, u. The vowel y never takes an accent.

(a.) *Accent aigu* ('), acute accent, over e only.
(b.) *Accent grave* (`), grave accent over a, e, u.
(c.) *Accent circonflexe* (^), circumflex accent, over a, e, i, o, u.

The other marks are: *Tréma* ("), diæresis, over e, i, u, when they are to be pronounced distinct from the preceding vowel.

Apostrophe ('), apostrophe, when a, e, i, are to be dropped before a following vowel.

Cédille (ç), cedilla, under the c only when it must be sounded as s, before a, o, or u.

Trait d'union (-), hyphen, which connects two or three words together.

III.—Pronunciation of Vowels.

1—*a bref* (short) is pronounced like *a* in *cat, chat* (pronounce *shah*).

2—*â long* (long, with a circumflex accent), or *a* followed by *s* is long, like in *arm*: *âme*, soul; *bras*, arm.

3—*a* is silent in *août*, August (pronounce *oo*); *toast* (like in English); *Saône*, river Saone (pronounce *sown*).

4—*e muet* (silent, *i.e.*, without accent), is hardly sounded in a word, something like *u* in *butter*.

5—*e muet*, is not sounded at all at the end of words of more than one syllable, like *e* in *mute*.

6—*e* is silent in Caen (pronounce *Khan*). See Nasal Sounds, 32.

7—*é fermé* (close, *i.e.*, with an acute accent) sounds like *y* in *vanity*, *vanité* in French.

8—*è ouvert* (open, *i.e.*, with a grave accent), like *e* in *where*: *près*, near.

9—*ê* (with a circumflex), like *ai* in the English word *air*: *être*, to be.

10—*i bref*, is sounded like *i* in *vanity*: *ici* (pronounce like the two English letters *e, c*), here.

11—*î long* (with a circumflex), like *ee* in *beet: île* (pronounce *eel*), island.
12—*i* is silent in *oignon* (onion), *moignon* (stump), *poignée* (handful), *poignet* (wrist), *poigne* (grip), *poignard* (dagger).
13—*o bref* (without accent), like *o* in *not: notre* (our).
14—*ô long* (with a circumflex), or *o* followed by *s*, like *o* in *no*, or *oa* in *boat: apôtre* (apostle), *gros* (big).
15—*o* is silent in *paon* (peacock), *faon* (fawn), *Laon* (Laon, a town in France), and *taon* (gadfly).
16—*u* has no corresponding sound in English; it sounds something like in *accurate, consecutive.*
17—*u* is not pronounced after *g*, except in *aiguille* (needle), *aiguiser* (to sharpen), *aiguillon* (goad), *aiguillonner* (to excite), *inextinguible* (inextinguishable), and the proper name *Guise*.
18—*y* after a vowel sounds like two *i*'s, *pays* (pai-is), country; but in all other cases like one *i*.

IV.—Diphthongs, and Combination of Vowels.

19—*ai*, final of verbs, is pronounced like *é: J'ai*, I have.
20—*ai*, followed by a consonant, and *ait*, are pronounced like *ai* in *air: faire*, to do, to make. N.B.—*ai* is sounded like *e* unaccented in this verb *faire*, when followed by *sant, sons, sais, sait, sions, siez, saient;* i.e., in the present participle, *faisant;* the first person plural of the present Indicative, *nous faisons;* and the whole of the imperfect Indicative.
21—*ais* and *aient*, are pronounced like long *ai* in *baiting; j'avais* (I had), *ils auraient* (they would have).
22—*au, eau, aud, aut*, and *aux*, are always long, and pronounced like *o* in *show*.
23—*Em, emn*, and *en* have the sound of *a* in *family*, in *femme* (woman), *indemnité* (indemnity), *hennir* (to neigh), *solennel* (solemn), and in all the adverbs of manner ending in *emment*.
24a—*er* (final of verbs of the first conjugation), *es, ed, et*, and *ier*, are pronounced like *é:—parler* (to speak), *vous-avez* (you have), *pied* (foot), *premier* (first), *soulier* (shoe), *panier* (basket), *jardinier* (gardener), *paquet* (parcel).

24b—*er*, not final of verbs, is sounded like *are* in *dare*: *fier* (proud), *hiver* (winter), *fer* (iron), *hier* (yesterday), *mer* (sea), *tender* (tender of a railway engine).

25—*es*, in monosyllables, is sounded like *è*: *des* (of the), *mes*, my.

26—*es*, in words of more than one syllable, is not sounded: *tables* (tables), *tu aimes* (thou lovest).

27—*ei*, and *ey*, in the middle or at the end of words, are sounded like *ei* in *leisure*: *enseigner* (to teach), *bey* (bey).

28—*elle, effe, esse, enne, erre, ette*—the first *e* is pronounced *è*, like in *elbow*, *chapelle* (chapel), *greffe* (graft), *paresse* (idleness), *antienne* (anthem), *pierre* (stone), *assiette* (plate); pronounce *cha-pè-l'*, *grè-f'*, *pa-rè-s'*, *an-ti-è-n'*, *piè-r'*, *a-ssiè-t'*.

29—*eu, œu, eux, œud*, and *œufs* (plural of *œuf*, egg), like *e* in *her;* except *eu* and *eus*, the past participle, and the past definite of the verb *avoir* (to have), which are pronounced *u*.

30—*Ou*, like *o* in *do*, or like two English *oo's*, as in *too*.

31—*oi*, like *oa* (the sound of the French *a* being short): *oiseau* (bird), pronounce *oa-zò*.

V.—Nasal Sounds.

32—*am, em* (before *b* and *p*), *an, aon*, and *ent*, are sounded like *en* in *encore*. N.B.—*Ent* is silent in verbs, when it is the termination of the third person *plural* of a tense.

33—*en*, in the body of words, is sounded like *an*: *entendre* (to hear); but like *in*, at the end of words: *examen* (examination), except in *abdomen*, *amen*, etc. (See § 72.)

34—*im, in, aim, ain*, are pronounced something like *en* in *length*. *In*, followed by a vowel, either at the beginning or at the end of a word, has the same sound as the English preposition *in*: *inutile* (useless), *cousine* (cousin), (*fem*.)

35—*imm* and *inn*, at the beginning of a word, are always followed by a vowel, and sounded as in English: *immortel* (immortal), *innombrable* (innumerable).

36—*om* and *on*, before a consonant, like *on* in *don't*. Before a vowel the *o* is pronounced separately, and the *m* or *n* is joined to the following vowel, like in English: *omelette* (*o-me-lette*), omelet; *onéreux* (*o-né-reux*), onerous.

VI.—Consonants.

B.

37—*um*, *un*, followed by a consonant, are sounded something like *un* in *hung* (the *g* being kept silent). When *un* is before a vowel the *u* makes a syllable, and the *n* is sounded with the following vowel: *unanime* (*u-na-nime*), unanimous.

38—B is silent in *plomb* (lead), but is sounded in *radoub* (refitting of a ship),* *club* (club), *rob* (rubber, at whist), and in proper names: *Joab*, *Job*, *Jacob*, etc. It is always pronounced when it is not final: *subtil* (subtile), *abjurer* (to abjure).

C.

39—C is hard before *a*, *o*, *u*, and soft before *e*, *i*, and *y*. With a cedilla it is always soft.

40—C final is generally sounded: *bec* (beak), *aqueduc* (aqueduct).

41—C final is not sounded in *accroc* (rent or tear), *ajonc* (furze), *banc* (form or bench), *blanc* (white), *broc* (jug or can), *clerc* (clerk), *cric* (screw-jack), *croc* (hook), *échecs* (chess), *escroc* (swindler), *estomac* (stomach), *flanc* (flank or side), *franc* (frank), *jonc* (rush), *lacs* (snare, gin), *marc* (residuum—*e.g.*, *marc de café*, grounds of coffee), *porc* (pork), *raccroc* (chance, lucky hit), *tabac* (tobacco), *tronc* (trunk of a tree).

42—C final is sounded in the singular *échec* (check); and in *donc* (then, therefore), when it begins a sentence. In all other cases it is not sounded, and *donc* is pronounced *don*.

43—C has the sound of *g* in *second* (second) and its derivatives.

44—CH is usually sounded as the English *sh*, but it has the sound of K in almost all words derived from the Greek, as: *archange* (archangel), *chœur* (choir), etc.; and in the word *yacht*.

45—CH is silent in *almanach* (almanack).

46—CT is silent in *respect* (respect, regard), *aspect* (aspect, sight, look), *instinct* (instinct), when followed by a consonant;

---

* According to the " Dictionnaire de l'Académie Française " the *b* is to be sounded in *radoub*; but Littré observes that sailors never sound it, even when it is followed by a vowel.

but if followed by a vowel the *c* is sounded like *k*; *e.g.*, aspect agréable, *aspek* agréable; respect affecté=*respek* affecté; instinct impérieux=*instink* impérieux. In the plural of these substantives *ct* is always silent: aspects agréables=*aspès* agréables; respects affectés=*respès* affectés; instincts impérieux=*instin-s*-impérieux.

D.

47—D final, which is usually silent, is sounded in *sud* (south), *éphod* (ephod, a part of the Jewish sacerdotal vestment), and in proper names: *David, Obed, Joad, Cid*.

48—D final, carried on to the next word, has the same sound as the hard T, as: *ce grand homme répond à tout* (that great man replies to everything), read: *ce grant homme répont à tout*.

49—D final in a substantive is not sounded on the following adjective, even if it begins with a vowel, as: *un froid extrême* (a very cold weather), read: *un froi extrême*; nor on the conjunctions *et* and *ou*, as: *le froid et le chaud* (cold and warm weather); *le chaud ou le froid* (warm or cold weather), read: le *froi* et le *chau*; le *chau* et le *froi*.

F.

50—F final is sounded like V in *neuf, dix-neuf, vingt-neuf*, etc., if the following noun or adjective begins with a vowel or *h* silent: *neuf hommes* (nine men) is pronounced *neuv-(h)ommes*. If the following noun or adjective begins with a consonant the *f* is silent: *neuf livres* (nine books) is pronounced *neu livres*.

51—F final is sounded in *canif* (penknife), and *neuf* (nine *or* new), numeral or qualificative adjective, at the end of a sentence, as: *Combien de plumes avez-vous? J'en ai neuf* (How many pens have you? I have nine). *J'ai un chapeau neuf* (I have a new hat).

52—F final is silent in *clef* (key), *chef-d'œuvre* (master-piece), *cerf* (stag), *un cerf-volant* (a kite), *un œuf frais* (a new-laid egg), *un œuf dur* (a hard-boiled egg), *le bœuf gras* (the fatted ox), *du bœuf salé* (salt beef), *des œufs* (some eggs), *des bœufs* (oxen), *les nerfs* (the nerves).

53—F final is sounded in *un chef* (a chief), *un bœuf* (an ox), *un œuf* (an egg), *un serf* (a slave).

G.

54—G final is usually silent.

55—G final is silent in the words formed with *bourg* and *berg*: *faubourg* (suburb), *Strasbourg*, *Spitsberg*, *Wurtemberg*, etc. Also in *coing* (quince), *étang* (pond), *rang* (rank), *sang* (blood), *long* (long), *poing* (fist), *hareng* (herring), *seing* (signature).

56—G final sounds like K before a vowel, as: *un rang élevé* (a high rank), *un sang illustré* (an illustrious family), are pronounced *un rank élevé*, *un sank illustre*; *suer sang et eau* (to toil and moil), is pronounced *suer sank et eau*.

57—G is silent in *doigt* (finger), *legs* (legacy), *sangsue* (leech), *vingt* (twenty), and its derivatives.

58—G before *e*, *i*, and *y* has the sound of *j* in *joue* (cheek), *jour* (day), as: *du gingembre* (some ginger).

59—G is sounded in *joug* (yoke), *grog* (grog), and *zigzag* (zigzag).

60—Gn at the beginning of words is pronounced like two different letters, as: *gnome*, pronounced *guenôme*.

61—Gn in a word is pronounced softly like the *g* in *signing*, as: *agneau* (lamb), *digne* (worthy), *régner* (to reign), *nous craignons* (we fear). But in the word *stagnation* and some few others both the *g* and *n* are sounded. In *signet* (book-maker), and in the proper names *Clugny*, *Regnaud*, and *Regnard*, the *g* is silent, and the *n* keeps its natural sound.

H.

62—H is either **silent**, as in *huître* (oyster), *habiter* (to dwell), *hésiter* (to hesitate), or **aspirate**, as in *haricot* (bean), *hibou* (owl), *héros* (hero). But *even when said to be* **aspirate**, *h is not* **breathed** *in French as in English*— that is to say, that to sound the *h* "*aspirate*," a simple hiatus is sufficient in French, as: *les héros* (the heroes), pronounce *lè-héros*, instead of *lèzéros*, as we pronounce *les hommes* (the men), *lèzommes*.

63—In the greater part of French words the *h* is silent; but there are nearly three hundred words in which it is aspirate. We only give here those which are most in use :—

Hache, axe.	*Hérisser*, to bristle up.
Hagard, haggard.	*Héros*, hero.
Haie, hedge.	*Hêtre*, beech-tree.
Haillon, rag.	*Heurter*, to strike against.
Haine, hatred.	*Hibou*, owl.
Halle, market-place.	*Hideux*, hideous.
Halte, halt.	*Hisser*, to hoist.
Haricot, bean.	*Homard*, lobster.
Harangue, speech.	*Honte*, shame.
Harasser, to harass.	*Hors*, out.
Hardi, bold.	*Houblon*, hops.
Hareng, herring.	*Houille*, coal.
Harnacher, to harness.	*Houle*, surge.
Harpe, harp.	*Houppe*, tuft.
Hasard, hazard.	*Housse*, saddle-cloth.
Hâte, haste.	*Houx*, holly.
Haut, high.	*Huit*, eight.
Havre, haven.	*Hurler*, to howl.
Hennir, to neigh.	*Hutte*, hut.
Héraut, herald.	

N.B.—If *h* is "aspirate" in a word in its simplest form, it is also in the derivatives, except in the case of *héros*, in the derivatives of which the *h* is silent, as *l'héroine* (the heroine), *l'héroïsme* (heroism). As for *huit*, the *h* becomes silent in *dix-huit* (eighteen), *soixante dix-huit* (seventy-eight), *quatre-vingt-dix-huit* (ninety-eight), and *vingt-huit* (twenty-eight)—pronounce *di-zuit*, and *vin-tuit*; but *h* is again "aspirate" in *quatre-vingt-huit* (eighty-eight).

L.

64—L liquid is always preceded by an *i*, either in the body or at the end of a word.

65—In a word, the *i* is followed by two *l*'s, the first of which is sounded like *l*, add the second like *y*, as in *bouteille* (bottle), pronounce *bouteil-ye*; *abeille*, (bee)=*abeil-ye*;

bouillir (to boil)=*bouil-yir*; *fille* (girl or daughter)=*fil-ye*; *famille* (family)=*famil-ye*.

66—At the end of a word the *i* is only followed by one *l*, which, however, is liquid, and sounded like the two *l*'s in the middle of the word, as: *ail* (garlic) = *ail-ye*; *travail* (work)=*travail-ye*; *camail* (a short cloak worn by cardinals, etc.) = *camail-ye*; *éventail* (fan) = *éventail-ye*; *soleil* (sun)=*soleil-ye*; *pareil* (alike)=*pareil-ye*; *orteil* (toe)=*orteil-ye*; *avril* (April)=*Avril-ye*; *babil* (prattle) = *babil-ye*; *mil* (millet) = *mil-ye*; *péril* (peril, danger) =*péril-ye*; *orgueil* (pride)=*orgueil-ye*; *fenouil* (fennel)= *fenouil-ye*; and most words ending in *ail*, *eil*, *ueil*, and *ouil*.

67—Exceptions : (1) *Ill* is not liquid at the beginning of words, as *illégal* (unlawful), *illégitime* (illegitimate), etc., etc., and at the end of some few others, such as *mille* (a thousand), *ville* (town).

68—(2) *L* is silent in *baril* (cask), *chenil* (kennel), *coutil* (ticking), *fils* (son), *fournil* (bake-house), *fusil* (gun), *gentil* (pretty), *gril* (gridiron), *outil* (tool), *persil* (parsley), *pouls* (pulse), *soûl* (drunk), *sourcil* (eyebrow), and in the plural *gentils-hommes* (noblemen).

69—L keeps its usual sound in *calme* (calm), *cil* (eyelash), *exil* (exile), *fil* (thread), *Nil* (Nile), *profil* (profile), *subtil* (subtile), *mil* (thousand, in dates of the Christian era), *civil* (courteous), *vil* (vile), *pupille* (pupil of the eye, or pupil, one under the care of a guardian), *distiller* (to distill), *vaciller* (to waver).

M.

70—M is silent in *automne* (autumn), *damner* (to curse), *condamner* (to condemn), *damnation* (damnation), *condamnation* (condemnation, sentence).

71—At the beginning of a word *emm* is nasal, as *emmener* (to take away), pronounce *en*-mener; *emmancher* (to fit a handle to)=*en*-mancher.

N.

72—N final is silent, but *abdomen*, *amen*, *Eden* are pronounced *abdomenn'*, *amenn'*, *Edenn'*. *Hymen* is pronounced either *imenn'* or *imain*.

P.

73—P is mute in *baptême* (baptism), *baptiser* (to baptise, to christen), *baptiste* (baptist), *compte* (account), *corps* (body), *dompter* (to tame, to subdue), *exempt* (exempt), *prompt* (quick), *sculpter* (to sculpture, to carve), *sculpteur* (sculptor), *sculpture* (sculpture), *sept* (seven), and at the end of words, except *cap* (cape), and *cep* (vine-plant).

74—P is sounded in *septembre* (September), *septuagénaire* (septuagenarian), *psaume* (psalm), *psalmiste* (psalmist), *psautier* (psalter), and some few others.

75—PH has the sound of f, as *philosophie* (philosophy), *phtisie* (consumption), etc.; pronounce *filosofie, ftisie*.

Q.

76—Q final is sounded in *coq* (cock) when used by itself, or when followed by a vowel, as: *un coq* (a cock), pronounced like in English; *un coq-à-l'âne* (cock-and-bull-story) = *un cokalâne*; but when the following word begins with a consonant the *q* is not sounded, as *coq d'inde* (turkey-cock), =*côdinde*. Q final is also sounded like a *K* in *cinq* (five), unless it is followed by a consonant, as: *Combien de plumes avez-vous? J'en ai cinq.* (How many pens have you? Five), pronounce *ceink*; but *cinq garçons* (five boys) pronounce *cein*. However, in the financial expression, *cinq pour cent* (five per cent.) the *q* is sounded.

77—When Q is not final, it is followed by *u*. It is generally pronounced like *k*, as *quand* (when)=*kan*; *quatre* (four)=*katre*; *querelle* (quarrel)=*kerelle*; *qui* (who)=*ki* (or in English *kee*; *que* (whom, or what)=*ke* or *keu*; *quel* (which or what)=*kel*.

78—But the *u* is sounded after *q* in *équestre* (equestrian), *équilatéral* (equilateral), *équitation* (riding, horsemanship), *quintuple* (five-fold), *questeur* (questor), *questure* (questorship).

79—Qu is pronounced *cou* in *aquatique* (aquatic), *équateur* (equator), *équation* (equation), *quadrupède* (quadruped), *quadruple* (four-fold), *in quarto*, etc.

R.

80—R final, which is usually sounded, is silent—

(a) In the termination—**er**, as: *le boucher* (the butcher), and in the infinitive of verbs of the first conjugation, as: *parler* (to speak).

(b) In the termination—**ier**, as: *l'officier* (the officer), *premier* (first), *écolier* (school-boy).

81—But it is sounded in—

MONOSYLLABLES, as: *hier* (yesterday), *mer* (sea), *fier* (proud); (but r is not sounded in the verb *fier* (to trust), which is properly composed of two syllables, and is pronounced *fi-é*).

82—DISSYLLABLES, as: *amer* (bitter), *auster* (south wind), *cancer* (cancer), *cuiller* (spoon), spelt also *cuillère*, *enfer* (hell), *éther* (ether), *thaler* (thaler).

83—R final is silent in the words (*Monsieur* and *Messieurs*), but is sounded in *sieur*.

84—Rн has always the sound of *R*, as in *rhume* (cold), *rhinocéros* (rhinoceros).

S.

85—S, when placed between two vowels, has the sound of *z*: (a) in the body of a word, as: *reposer* (to rest), pronounce *reposé*; and (b) at the end of a word when carried on to the next word beginning with a vowel or *h* silent, as: *mes amis* (my friends), pronounce *mé-zamis*.

86—But S has its usual sound in compound words, when the simple word begins with *s* as *vraisemblable* (likely) = *vrai-semblable*.

87—S final, which is generally silent, is sounded in—

Albinos, albino.
Aloès, aloes.
Atlas, atlas.
As, ace.
Blocus, investment (of a town), blockade (of a port).
Calus, callosity.
Iris, iris, rainbow.
Laps, lapse.
Lis, lily, but silent in *fleur-de-lis*.
Maïs, maize.
Mérinos, merino.
Omnibus, omnibus.
Plus-que-parfait, pluperfect.
Prospectus, prospectus.
Rhinocéros, rhinoceros.
Tournevis, screw-driver.
Vasistas (pronounce *vazistas*), casement window.
Vis, screw;

and some others not often met with.

N.B.—In *ours* (bear) a great many people pronounce the *s*.

88—It is also sounded in words adopted from the Latin, as: *bis* (twice, encore!) *chorus*, *gratis*, *hiatus*, *oremus* (oremus, prayer), *sinus* (sinus), and in proper names (Latin or Greek) such as *Bacchus*, *Crésus*, *Cyrus*, *Minos*, *Pallus*, *Sémiramis*. [N.B.—S final is not sounded in *bis* (brown), as: *du pain bis* (brown bread), pronounce *bee*.]

The final *s* is not sounded before a consonant in *Denis*, *Jésus*, *Judas*, *Mathias*, *Nicholas*, *Paris*, *Thomas*.

89—S final is sounded like *z* in *obus* (shell).

90—S final is not sounded on the following vowel in the second person singular of the present indicative and subjunctive, as: *tu aimes à jouer* (thou likest to play); *il faut que tu ailles à l'école* (thou must go to school); pronounce *tu aim⌢à jouer*; *tu aill⌢à l'école*.

91—Sc is sounded like *s* in *scène* (scene, stage) = *sên'*; *scénique* (scenical) = *sénik*; *sceptique* (sceptic) = *sè-ptik*; *science* (science) = *si-ans'*, and some other words.

T.

92—T at the beginning of words has the same sound as in English, even when it is followed by two vowels, as *le tiers*, the third.

93—T in the middle of words, when followed by the vowel *i*, is sometimes pronounced like *t*, and sometimes like *s*:

I. Like *t*:—

(a) In all words where it is preceded by *s* or *x*, as *bastion* (bastion), *bestial* (beastly), *digestion* (digestion), *mixtion* (mixture), *question* (question).

(b) In all words ending in *tié* or *tier*, as *amitié* (friendship), *moitié* (half), *charpentier* (carpenter), *châtier* (to chastise); except in the two verbs *balbutier* (to lisp) and *initier* (to initiate), and all its derivatives, where *t* is pronounced like *s*.

(c) In words ending in *tie*, as *partie* (part), *modestie* (modesty), etc., except in *facétie* (facetiousness), *ineptie* (silliness), *inertie* (sluggishness), *minutie* (trifle), *prophétie* (prophecy); and in words ending in *atie*, as *démocratie* (democracy), where *t* has the sound of *s*.

(d) In words ending in *tien* and *tienne*, as *Chrétien* (Christian), *maintien* (maintenance), *soutien* (support), *que je tienne* (that I may hold), *antienne* (anthem); except in proper names, as *Dioclétien* (Diocletian), and adjectives denoting nationality, as *Vénitien Vénitienne* (Venetian), where *t* is sounded like *s*.

(e) In all the persons of verbs ending in *tions* and *ties*, as: *nous partions, vous parties* (we were, you were starting); *nous portions* (we were carrying), but the substantive *portions* (portions) is pronounced *porsions*.

II. Like *s*:—

(a) In the word *patient* (patient), and all its derivatives.

(b) In words ending in *tial, tiel, tion*, as *partial* (partial), *confidentiel* (confidential), *admiration* (admiration), *nation* (nation).

(c) In some words ending in *tie* and in all substantives ending in *atie* [see above, I. (c)].

(d) In the words *satiété* (satiety), *insatiable* (insatiable).

94—T final is silent, except when followed by another word beginning with a vowel, as *est-elle* (is she), *tout-à-fait* (quite entirely); *but it is* ALWAYS SILENT *in the conjunction* et, *and*.

T final is sounded in the following words: *Brut* (raw, uncultivated), *Christ* (Christ), *chut!* (hush!), *contact* (contact), *correct* (correct), *dot* (dowry), *direct* (direct), *exact* (punctual, exact), *est* (east), *fat* (fop), *granit* (granite),* *incorrect* (incorrect), *indirect* (indirect), *inexact* (inaccurate), *infect* (infectious), *intact* (untouched, intact), *knout* (knout), *lest* (ballast), *échec et mat* (checkmate), *net* (clear, clean, net), *ouest* (west), *rit* or *rite* (rite), *strict* (strict), *toast* or *toste* (toast) *ut* (or *do*, the note C in music), *whist* (whist).

95—In *sept* (seven) and *huit* (eight) the *t* is silent when the following word begins with a consonant or *h* aspirate, as: *sept haches* (seven axes), *sept francs* (seven francs), *huit couteaux* (eight knives) = *sé haches*, etc.

* Also pronounced grani(t).

96 — In *vingt* the *t* is sounded before a vowel, and in all numbers from 21 to 29, as *vingt-et-un, vingt-deux, vingt-trois,* etc. It is mute in all other cases. (See N. B., § 63.)

Th.

97 — Th at the beginning, in the middle, and at the end of words, is sounded like *t*, as: *théâtre* (theatre), *méthode* (method), *Judith* (Judith), *Goliath* (Goliath), *Ruth* (Ruth), *luth* (lute); pronounce *teâtr', métod', Judit',* etc.

98 — Th is not pronounced in *asthme* (asthma) and *asthmatique* (asthmatic); pronounce *azm', azmatik.*

V.

99 — V has exactly the same sound in French as in English, as *vanité* (vanity).

W.

100 — W is sounded like in English in words taken from that language, as *wagon* (railway carriage), *warrant, waterproof, Wesleyen, Whig, whiskey, whist, wigwam,* etc.

101 — W has the sound of V in words taken from the German and Northern languages, as *Westphalie, Wagram, Wasa.*

X.

102(a) — X final is generally silent; when followed by a word beginning with a vowel or an h mute it is joined like *s* (85, b.).

102(b) — X has the sound of *cs* in *Alexandre* (Alexander), *extrême* (extreme), *maxime* (maxim), *luxe* (luxury), *sexe* (sex):

103 — Of Gz in *exercice* (exercise), *examen* (examination), and when it is between two vowels in a word beginning with *in* as *inexact* (inaccurate); also in proper names, as *Le Xant-, Xantippe, Xavier, Xercès:*

104 — Of Ss in *Bruxelles* (Brussels), *Auxerre,* and *Aix-en-Provence, soixante* (sixty):

105 — Of Ks in :—

(a) *excepter* (to except), *excellent* (excellent), *exception* (exception), *excès* (excess), *exciter* (to excite).

(b) at the end of the words *index, larynx, lynx, phénix, préfix* (prefixed), *thorax,* etc., although *x* final is not generally sounded, as *animaux* (animals), pronounce *animô.*

(c) At the end of proper names, as *Ajax, Pollux, Fairfax, Styx*, etc.:

106—Of Z in *deuxième* (second), *sixième* (sixth), *dixième* (tenth); and at the end of a word when followed by a vowel, as, *de beaux yeux* (fine eyes), pronounce *bô-zieû*.

107—X final is not sounded in *deux* (two), *six* (six), and *dix* (ten), when the noun they multiply follows them, and begins with a consonant or *h* aspirate, as *deux femmes* (two women), *six haches* (six axes), *dix pommes* (ten apples).

108—When *six* and *dix* are not followed by the noun which they multiply, the final *x* has the sound of double *s*, as: *Avez-vous dix livres? Non, j'en ai six* (Have you ten books? No, I have six), pronounce *dee* and *siss*. But if the noun which they multiply follows them and begins with a vowel or *h* silent, *x* is sounded like *z* in *deux*, *six*, and *dix*, as *deux amis* (two friends), *six oranges* (six oranges), *dix hommes* (ten men); pronounce *deu-zamis*, etc. The same for *dix-sept* (seventeen), *dix-huit* (eighteen), *dix-neuf* (nineteen)=*dis*.

Z.

109—Z final is not sounded before a following consonant, except in the word *gaz* (gas).

110—Z final sounds like a hard *s* in *Metz* (pronounced *Messe*), *Rodez, Suez*, and proper names, as *Alvarez, Cortez*.

111—In the following list letters printed in *italics* are not to be pronounced:—

Ca*en* (Caen),	pronounce	Kan.
S'*as*seoir (to sit down),	,,	A-soir.
La*on* (Laon),	,,	Lan.
Pa*on* (peacock),	,,	Pan.
Fa*on* (fawn),	,,	Fan.
Fi*ls* (son),*	,,	Fi.
Blan*c* (white),	,,	Blan.
Mon*s*ieur (sir).	,,	Mo-ssieu.
Pou*ls* (pulse),	,,	Poû.
Estoma*c* (stomach),	,,	Estoma.

* A great many people pronounce the *s* in *fils*.

Toast (toast),	pronounce	Tôst.
Août (August),	,,	Oû.
Franc (frank),	,,	Fran.
Clef (key),	,,	Clé.
Goth (Goth),	,,	Gô.
Al-ma-nach (almanac),	,,	Al-ma-na.
Domp-té (subdued),	,,	Don-té.
Joie (joy),	,,	Joî.
Sang-sue (leech),	,,	San-sû.
Oi-gnon (onion),	,,	O-gnon.
Dé-voue-ment (devotedness)	,,	Dé-vou-ment.
Il niera (he will deny),	,,	Il ni-ra.
Saône (river Saone)	,,	Sône.
Taon (ox-fly)	,,	Tan.

The final letters in such words as the following are to be pronounced *only* when they are followed by a vowel or *h* silent :

Bout (end).	(ils) Pen-sent † (they think).
Es-prit (mind).	Pe-tit (small).
Gens (people).	Plus (more).
Heu-reux (happy).	Pot (pot).
Hon-teux * (ashamed).	Rang (rang).
Long (long).	Sang (blood).
Mais (but).	Saint (holy).
Mè-res (mothers).	Tout (all).
Mont (mount).	Tiers (third).
Pè-res (fathers).	(tu) Tiens (thou holdest).
Paix (peace).	(il) Vient (he comes).

* And in all the adjectives ending in *eux*.
† This applies to *all* verbs.

N.B.—We are indebted to Messrs. BRETTE & MASSON for the above hints on French pronunciation.

PREMIÈRE PARTIE.
FIRST PART.

L'ALPHABET.—THE ALPHABET.

Majuscules.—Capital Letters.

A B C D E F G H I J
K L M N O P Q R S T
U V W X Y Z

A B C D E F G H I J K
L M N O P Q R S T U
V W X Y Z

𝒜 ℬ 𝒞 𝒟 ℰ ℱ 𝒢 ℋ ℐ 𝒥
𝒦 ℒ ℳ 𝒩 𝒪 𝒫 𝒬 ℛ 𝒮 𝒯
𝒰 𝒱 𝒲 𝒳 𝒴 𝒵

L'ALPHABET.—THE ALPHABET.

Minuscules.—Small Letters.

a b c d e f g h i j k l
m n o p q r s t u v w
x y z

a b c d e f g h i j k l
m n o p q r s t u v w
x y z

a b c d e f g h i j k l m n o p
q r s t u v w x y z

A ah	F eff	K kah	P pay	U u	Z zed
B bay	G jay	L ell	Q qu	V vay	
C say	H ash	M emm	R air	W doublevay	
D day	I ee	N enn	S ess	X eeks	
E er	J jee	O o	T tay	Y e-grek	

Sons ou Voyelles Simples.—Simple Sounds.

A a *a*
p*a*p*a*, *papa.*

 Â â â
â-ne, *ass.*

E e *e*
d*e*-mi, *half.*

É é *é*
é-té, *summer.*

È è *è*
m*è*-re, *mother.*

Ê ê *ê*
t*ê*-te, *head.*

I i *i*
i-ma-ge, *image.*

Î î *î*
î-le, *island.*

Y y *y*
l*y*-re, *lyre.*

O o *o*
*o*r, *gold.*

Ô ô *ô*
c*ô*-té, *side.*

U u *u*
m*u*-let, *mule.*

Û û *û*
m*û*-re, *mulberry.*

Sons Simples représentés par plus d'une Voyelle.

Simple Sounds represented by more than one Vowel.

Au	Chaud *hot.*	Faux *scythe.*
Eau	Eau *water.*	A-gneau *lamb.*
Eu	Feu *fire.*	Heu-reux *happy.*
Ou	Chou *cabbage.*	Jou-jou *plaything.*

Diphthongues.—Diphthongs.

Ia	Piano	*Piano*
Ie	Pied	*Foot*
Io	Pioche	*Pickaxe*
Oi	Roi	*King*
Ui	Hui-le	*Oil*
Ui	Suif	*Tallow*
Oui	Oui	*Yes*

Sons Nasaux.—Nasal Sounds.

An	An *year.*	Fan-tôme *ghost.*
En	En *in.*	En-fant *child.*
In	Fin *end.*	En-fin *at last.*
On	Bon *good.*	Bon-bon *sweetmeat.*
Un	Un *one.*	Cha-cun *each.*
Ain	Pain *bread.*	Étain *tin.*
Aim	Faim *hunger.*	Daim *deer.*

SECONDE PARTIE.—SECOND PART.

Un Â-ne.   *An Ass.*
Un Â-non.   *A young Ass.*

Le Che-val.   *The Horse.*
Le Ca-va-li-er.   *The Rider.*

Le Cy-gne.
Le long Cou.

The Swan.
The long Neck.

Un Pois-son.
Les Na-geoi-res.

A Fish.
The Fins.

Le Chat.
Grif-fer.

The Cat.
To Scratch.

La Sou-ris.
La Sou-ri-ci-è-re.

The Mouse.
The Mouse-trap.

Le Bœuf.   The Ox.
Les Cor-nes. The Horns.

Le Mou-ton.   The Sheep.
La Ber-gè-re. The Shepherdess.

Le Lion.   *The Lion.*
La Cri-ni-è-re.   *The Mane.*

Le Pont.   *The Bridge.*
La Ri-vi-è-re.   *The River.*

Le Hi-bou.   The Owl.
Deux Hi-boux.   Two Owls.

Un Nid.   A Nest.
Un Oi-seau.   A Bird.

Le Re-nard.
La Queue touf-fue.

The Fox.
The bushy Tail.

Le Liè-vre.
La Ti-mi-di-té.

The Hare.
The Timidity.

Un Ours.   *A Bear.*
La Nei-ge.   *The Snow.*

La Mai-son.   *The House.*
La por-te et les fe-nê-tres.   *The Door and the Windows*

L'É-gli-se.   The Church.
La Tour.   The Tower.

Le Li-vre.   The Book.
La Pa-ge.   The Page.

Le Chien.
La Fi-dé-li-té.

The Dog.
Fidelity.

Un Pa-nier.
Le grand Panier.

A Basket.
The big Basket.

Le Coq.
La Crê-te.

The Cock.
The Comb.

La Chè-vre.
L'En-fant.

The Goat.
The Child.

D

Un La-pin.   *A Rabbit.*
Un La-pin blanc.   *A white Rabbit.*

Un Ber-ceau.   *A Cradle.*
Le Bé-bé.   *The Baby.*

La Pou-le.   The Hen.
Les Pou-lets. The Chickens.

La Brou-et-te. The Wheelbarrow.
Le Mou-lin.   The Mill.

Un Ar-bre.   *A Tree.*
Les Bran-ches.   *The Branches.*

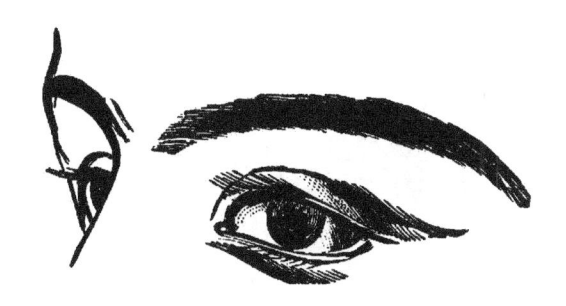

L'Oeil.   *The Eye.*
Les Y-eux.   *The Eyes.*

La Ta-ble.
Le Pied de la Table.

The Table.
The Leg of the Table.

Un Tambour.
Le Bruit.

A Drum.
The Noise.

La Ru-che.   The Bee-hive.
L'A-beil-le.   The Bee.

Une Pou-pée.   A Doll.
La Robe et le Cha-peau.   The Dress and the Hat.

L'Au-ber-ge.   The Inn.
L'É-cu-rie.   The Stable.

Le Ca-nard.   The Duck.
Le Bec.   The Beak.

La Clo-che.   The Bell.
Le Battant.   *The Clapper.*

Un Ba-teau.   *A Boat.*
Le Pa-ra-plu-ie.   *The Umbrella.*

La Frai-se.
Les bon-nes Frai-ses.

The Strawberry.
The good Strawberries.

Un Vais-seau.
La Mer.

A Ship.
The Sea.

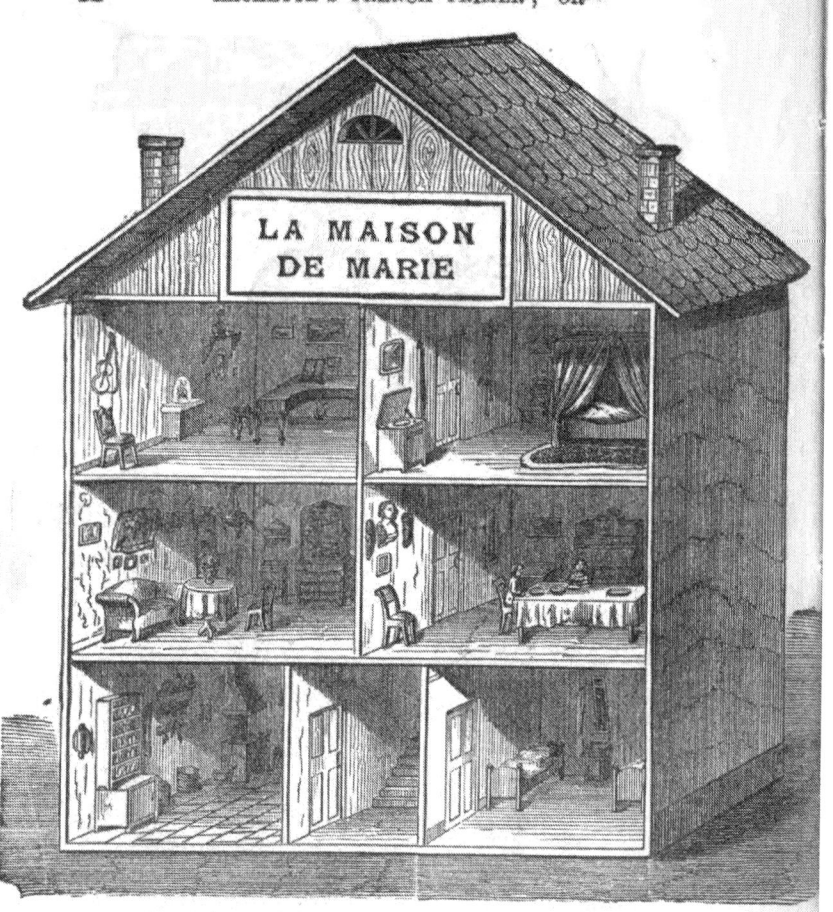

La Mai-son de Ma-rie.
The   House   of   Mary.

Mary's House.

Le Toit.   *The Roof.*
La Che-mi-née.   *The Chimney.*

La Maison de Marie.

Mary's House.

La por-te.	*The door.*
Le pas-sa-ge.	*The passage.*
La cu-i-si-ne.	*The kitchen.*
La cham-bre.	*The room.*
La cham-bre à cou-cher.	*The bedroom.*
L'es-ca-li-er.	*The staircase.*
Le sa-lon.	*The drawing room.*
La sal-le.	*The hall.*
La sal-le à man-ger.	*The dining-hall.*
La nap-pe.	*The cloth.*
L'é-tu-de.	*The study.*
Le pi-a-no.	*The piano.*
Le lit.	*The bed.*
Les ri-deaux.	*The curtains.*

Please to tell me the English for:—

Oreille, grenouille, chasse, souris, cornes, pont, nid, église, chien, berceau, œil, brouette, tambour, canard, ruche, fraise, bateau, toit, cuisine, escalier, nappe, lit, rideaux.

I should like to know the French for:—

Baby, scissors, watch, father, cock, rabbit, mill, tree, horse, fish, ox, tail, basket, door, passage, room, drawing-room, study, sword, spoon.

TROISIÈME PARTIE.

THIRD PART.

La cuil-ler de bébé.

Baby's spoon.

Char-les a un fu-sil
Charles has a gun

et un sa-bre.
and a sword.

Ce-ci est une
This   is   an
o-reil-le.
ear.

Voi-ci le dé et
Here are the thimble and
les ciseaux.
the   scissors.

Pre-nez ce ver-re.
Take   this   glass.

La mon-tre de pa-pa.
Papa's watch.

Les gre-nouil-les sau-tent.
The frog's jump.

Le puits est pro-fond.
The well is deep.

Ceci est une
This is a
ca-ra-fe.
decanter.

Le cer-ceau est
The hoop is
rond.
round.

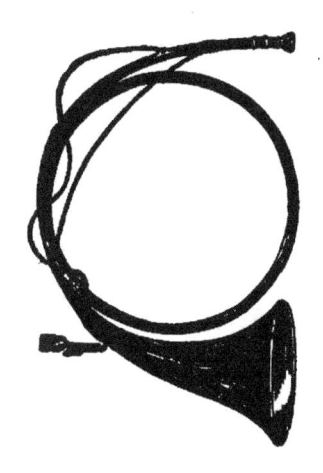

Mon pè-re a un
My father has a
cor de chas-se.
hunting-horn.

L'a-rai-gnée et
The   spider   and

sa toi-le.
its   webb.

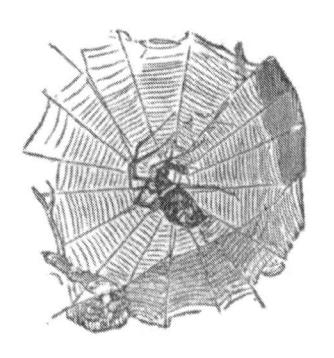

L'ar-ro-soir pour
The watering pot   for

les fleurs.
the   flowers.

Voi-là une
There is   a

feuil-le.
leaf.

Voi-ci des glands
Here are   some   acorns
tom-bés d'un
fallen   from an
chê-ne.
oak.

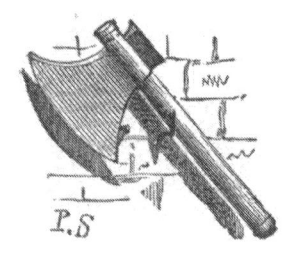

La ha-che pour
The   axe   to
coup-er le chê-ne.
cut down the   oak.

La roue de la
The wheel of the
voi-tu-re.
carriage.

Quel jo-li pe-tit
What a pretty little
   oi-seau !
    bird !

Le coq gron-de la
The cock scolds the
   pou-le.
    hen.

La va-che don-ne
The cow gives
   de bon lait.
   some good milk.

Voi-ci des quil-les.
Here are   skittles.

Un en-fant sau-vé
A   child   saved
par un chi-en.
by   a   dog.

Déf-i-ez-vous,
Beware
pe-ti-tes sou-ris
little   mice

Cru-el-le sé-pa-ra-ti-on.
Painful   separation.

La main a qua-tre doigts et
The hand has   four   fingers and

un pou-ce.
a   thumb.

Le re-nard est très ru-sé.
The fox is very sly.

Le cor-beau est très noir.
The crow is very black.

Le mout-on a un a-gneau.
The sheep has a lamb.

Les gar-çons ont une bal-le.
The boys have a ball.

Est-il ar-ri-vé un ac-ci-dent au
Has an accident happened to the
cha-ri-ot ?
waggon ?

Voy-ez le pe-tit chien sur le si-è-ge.
See the little dog on the box.

Le meu-ni-er et son â-ne
The   miller   and his   ass

é-cou-tent le tam-bour.
listen to   the   drum.

Bé-bé est dans son ber-ceau.
Baby   is   in   its   cradle.

Le pè-re gron-de son fils.
The father scolds his son.

Ils ren-trent la mois-son.
They are taking the harvest home.

Le pau-vre li-è-vre se-ra-t-il pris?
Will the poor hare be taken?

Le chas-seur part pour la chas-se.
The sportsman is going out shooting.

Ce-ci est un mou-lin à eau.
This is a water mill.

Un che-val libre et heu-reux.
A horse free and happy.

Le ca-pi-tai-ne a ti-ré son sa-bre.
The captain has drawn his sword.

Un nou-veau ré-gi-ment.
A new regiment.

Le bû-che-ron est fort;
The woodcutter is strong;
il a-bat l'ar-bre.
he cuts down the tree.

L'é-tang dans la fo-rêt.
The pond in the forest.

Quel est le plus en-tê-té des
Which is the most obstinate of the

deux ?
two ?

Le chat n'est pas là !
The cat is not there!

Ces trois ca-nards ai-ment
These three ducks like

beau-coup l'eau ; ils ont de
the water very much ; they have

l'eau de tous les cô-tés.
water on all sides.

Le châ-teau du sei-gneur est
The   lord's castle   is

en-tou-ré d'un fos-sé très
surrounded   by a   very

lar-ge.
broad moat.

Le pau-vre pri-son-ni-er est très
The poor prisoner is very

mal-heu-reux dans ce vi-lain
unhappy in this ugly

ca-chot.
dungeon.

Je vou-drais bi-en de-meu-rer
I should like to live

dans cet-te mai-son au bord
in this house on the bank

du lac.
of the lake.

L'o-ra-ge va bi-en-tôt
The storm   is soon going to

é-cla-ter sur cet-te hau-te
burst   on   this   high

mon-ta-gne.
mountain.

A quoi pen-sent ces deux hi-boux?
What are these two owls thinking of?

Je vou-drais le sa-voir; et vous
I should like to know; and you

aus-si, n'est-ce pas?
too, would you not?

Je ne vou-drais pas ren-con-trer
I should not like to meet

ce mon-sieur.
this gentleman.

Quatrième Partie.

Fourth Part.

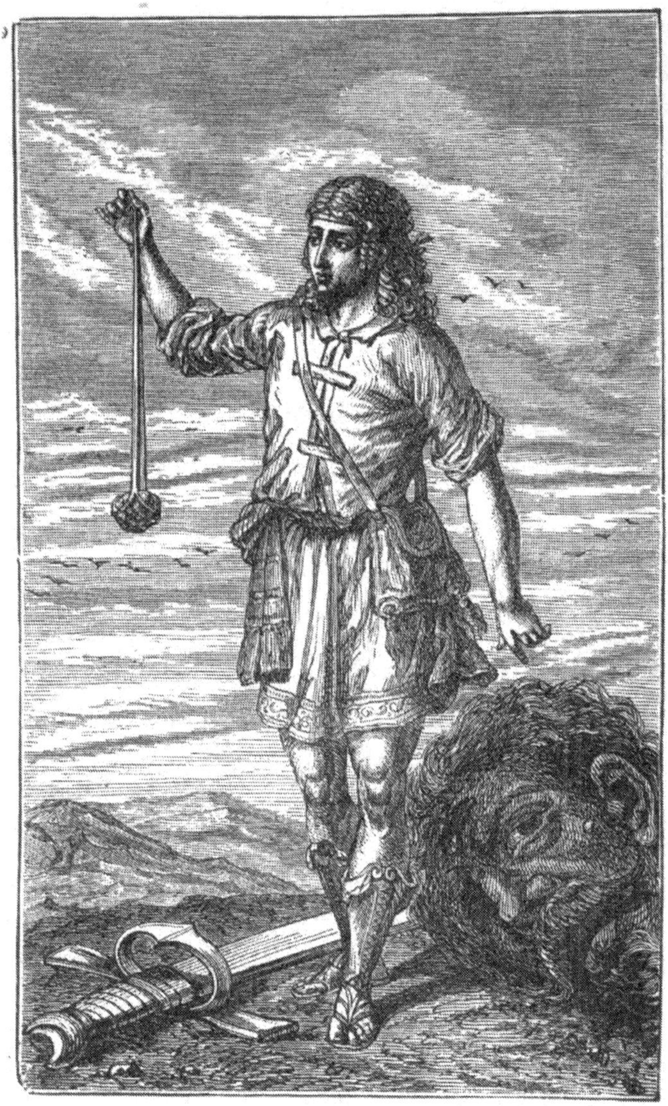

Les Parties du Corps.
The Parts of the Body.

La tête ; le bras, les bras ;
The head ; the arm, the arms ;

la jambe, les jambes ; la main,
the leg, the legs ; the hand,

les mains ; le pied, les pieds ;
the hands ; the foot, the feet ;

les cheveux ; le front ; l'œil,
the hair ; the forehead ; the eye,

les yeux ; le nez ; la bouche ;
the eyes ; the nose ; the mouth ;

le menton ; l'oreille, les oreilles.
the chin ; the ear, the ears.

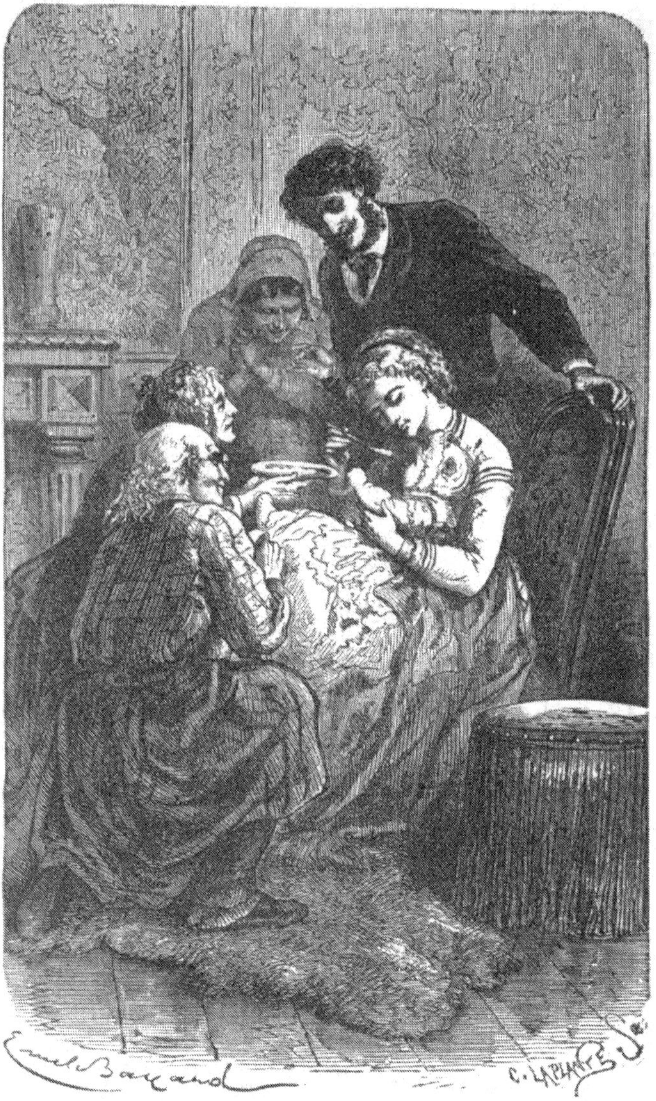

Tout le monde aime bébé,
Everybody loves baby,

son père, sa mère, son grand-
its father, its mother, its grand-

père, sa grand'mère et sa
father, its grandmother and its

nourrice. La maman fait
nurse. The mother

manger bébé, et tous les
feeds baby, and all the

autres le regardent pendant
others look at it whilst

qu'il mange. Bébé ne parle
it is eating. Baby does not speak

pas encore.
yet.

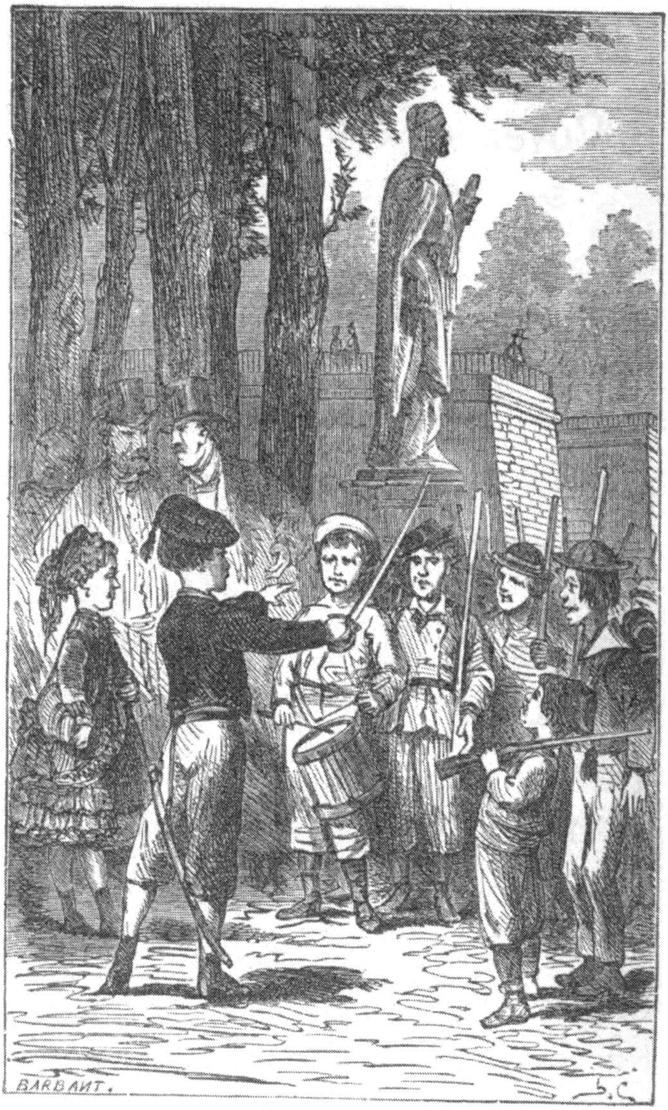
BARBANT.

Voyez ce beau régiment de
See that fine regiment of

braves soldats! Le capitaine
brave soldiers! The captain

a un sabre. Les soldats ont
has a sword. The soldiers have

des fusils. Louis est tambour;
guns. Lewis is drummer;

il a un tambour et des
he has a drum and some

baguettes.
drumsticks.

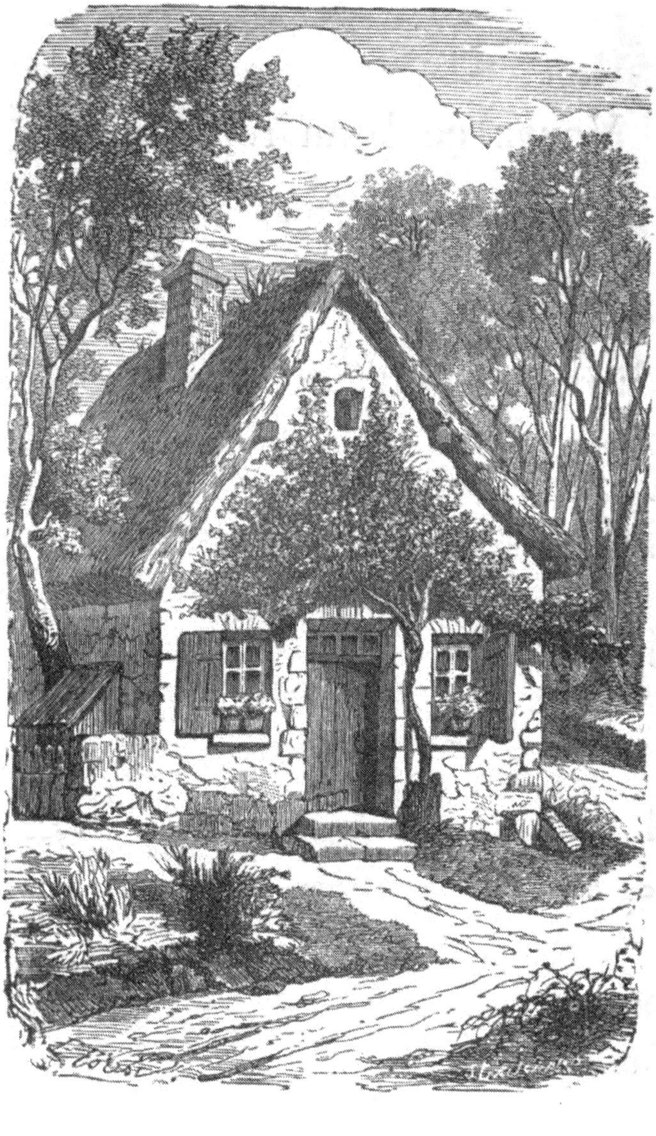

Voici le cottage de la
Here is the   cottage   of

nourrice d'Ernest. Il est
Ernest's nurse.   It   is

couvert en chaume. La porte
covered with thatch. The door

est entr'ouverte. Il y a deux
is   ajar.   There are two

fenêtres sur le devant et une
windows at the front and an

lucarne. Il y a deux marches
attic window. There are two steps

devant la porte.
before the door.

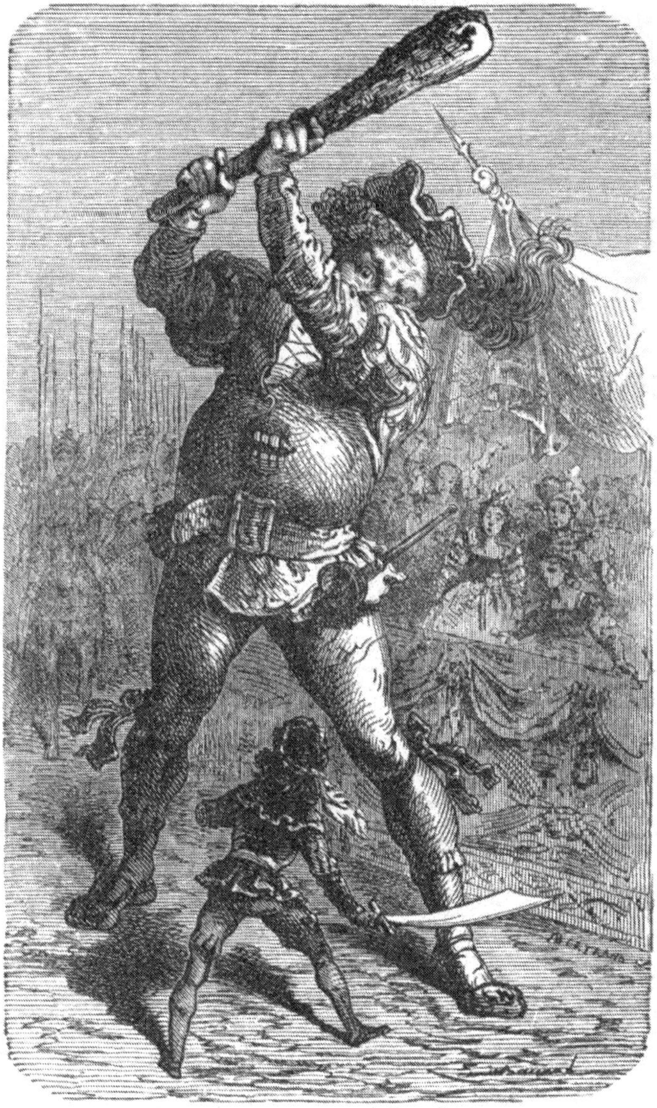

Voyez ce grand géant; il
See that great giant; he

est en colère; il a une
is angry; he has a

grande massue; il veut tuer
great club; he wishes to kill

"Jack"; mais "Jack" est
Jack; but Jack is

brave, il a un bon sabre;
brave, he has a good sword;

il tuera le géant. Vive
he will kill the giant. Hurrah! for

"Jack!"
Jack.

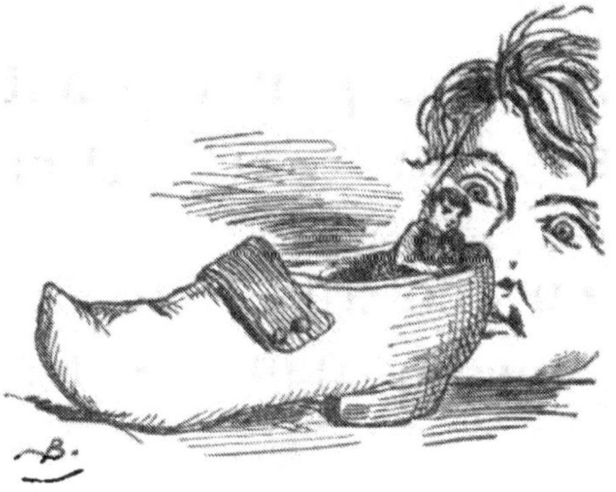

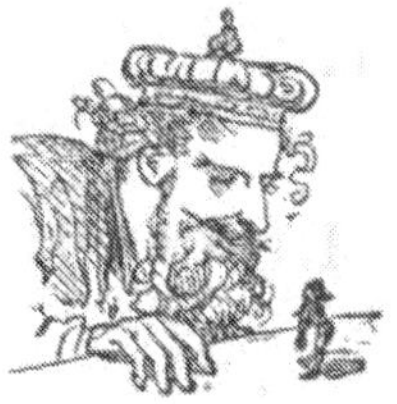

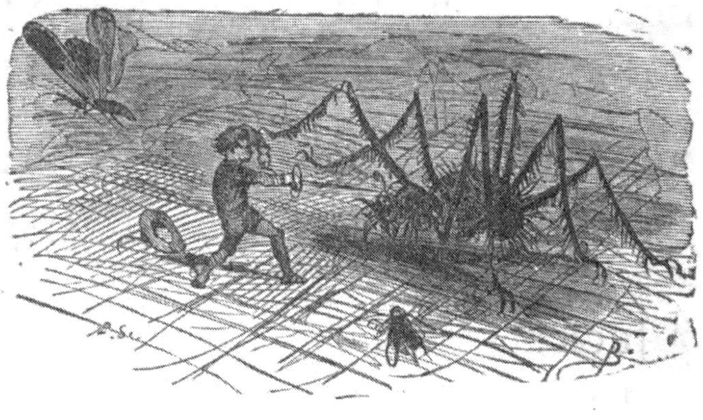

Tom Pouce est très petit.
Tom Thumb is very small.

Il demeure dans un sabot.
He lives in a wooden shoe.

Il a été présenté au roi.
He has been presented to the king.

Tom Pouce est très brave.
Tom Thumb is very brave.

Il se bat contre une grosse araignée.
He fights against a large spider.

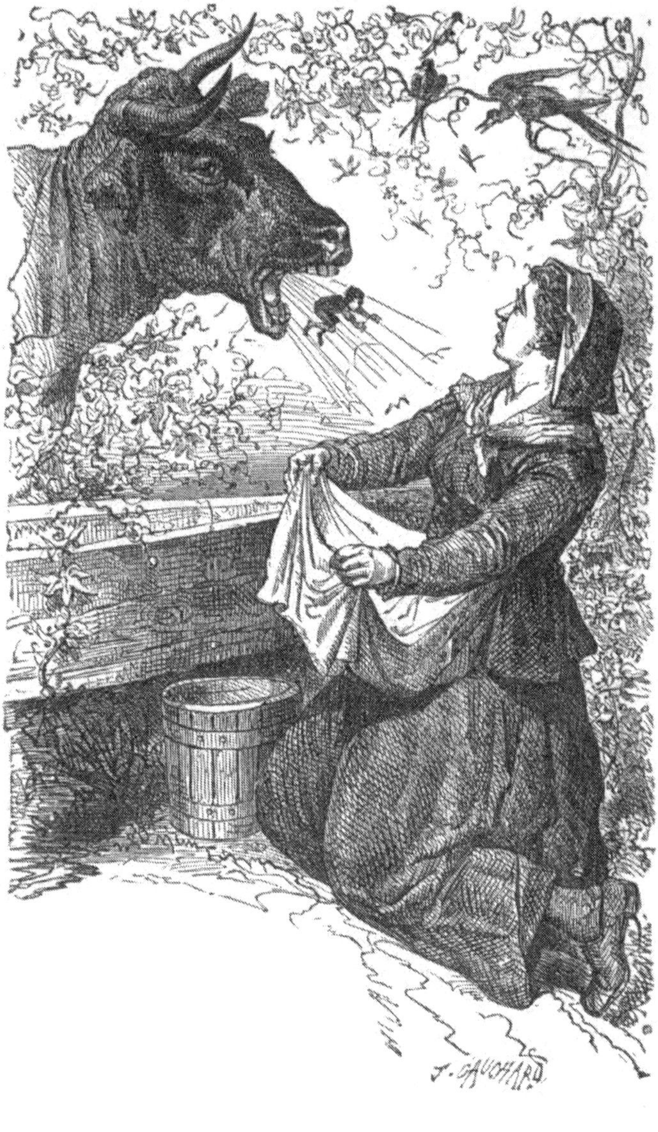

La vache a avalé le pauvre
The cow has swallowed poor

Tom Pouce ; il est si
Tom Thumb; he is so

petit. Mais Tom n'est pas
small. But Tom is not

mort ; voyez, la vache le
dead; see, the cow gives

rend à sa maman qui est
him back to his mamma who is

bien contente.
very much pleased.

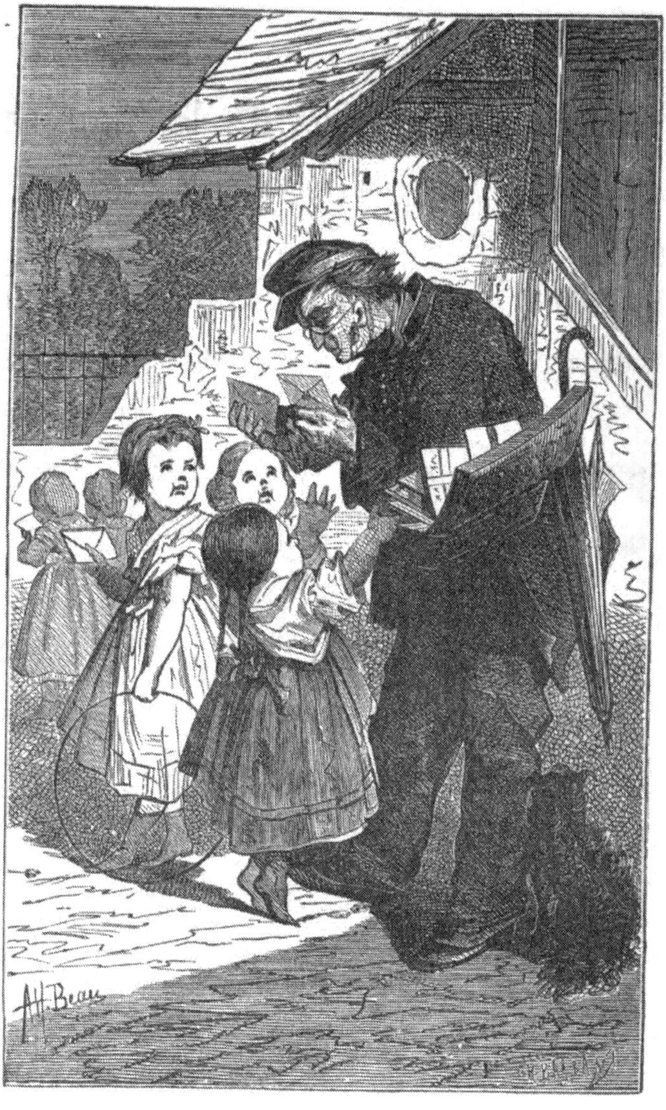

Le facteur apporte des
The postman brings some

lettres. Il les prend dans
letters. He takes them from

sa boîte et les donne aux
his box and gives them to the

petits enfants qui vont les
little children who are going to

porter à leur papa et à leur
take them to their papa and to their

maman.
mamma.

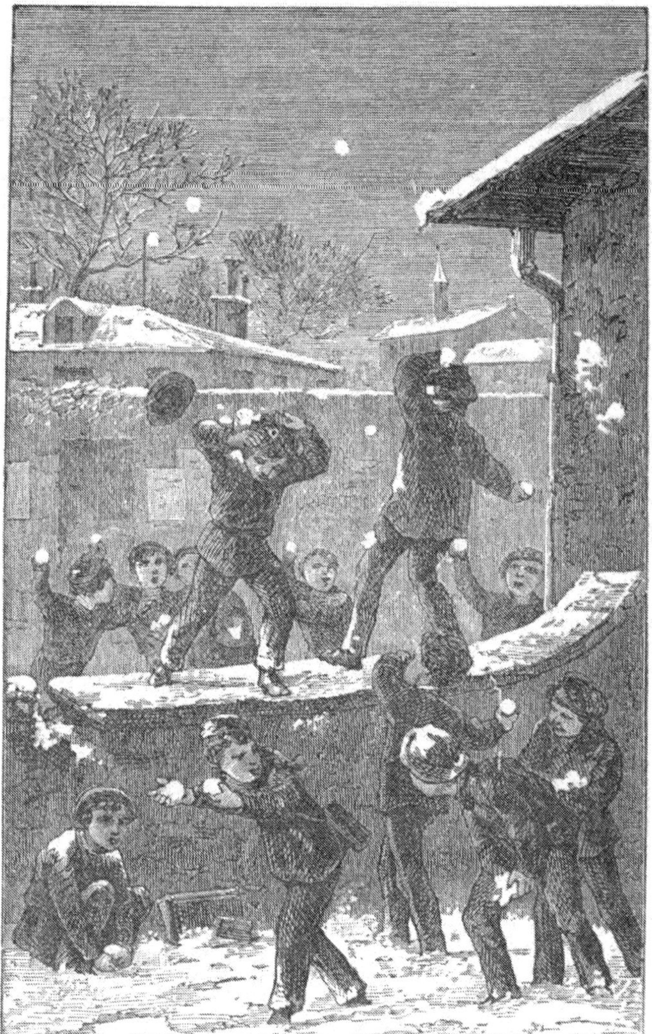

Nous sommes en hiver. Il
We   are   in   winter. There

y a de la neige et les enfants
is some   snow and the   children

au sortir de l'école font des
on going out of school   make

boules de neige et se les
snow balls   and throw them

jettent. Il y a deux garçons
at one another. There are two   boys

sur le mur.
on the wall.

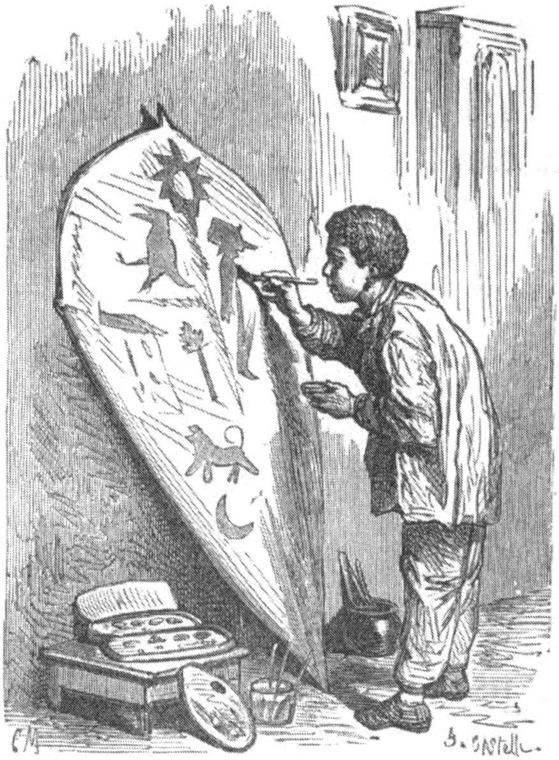

Georges est très adroit. Il
George is very clever. He

a fait ce cerf-volant lui-même.
has made this kite himself.

Le cerf-volant est plus grand
The kite is taller

que Georges. L'artiste a
than George. The artist has

peint une maison, un petit
painted a house, a little

chien, un homme, la lune et
dog, a man, the moon, and

un oiseau.
a bird.

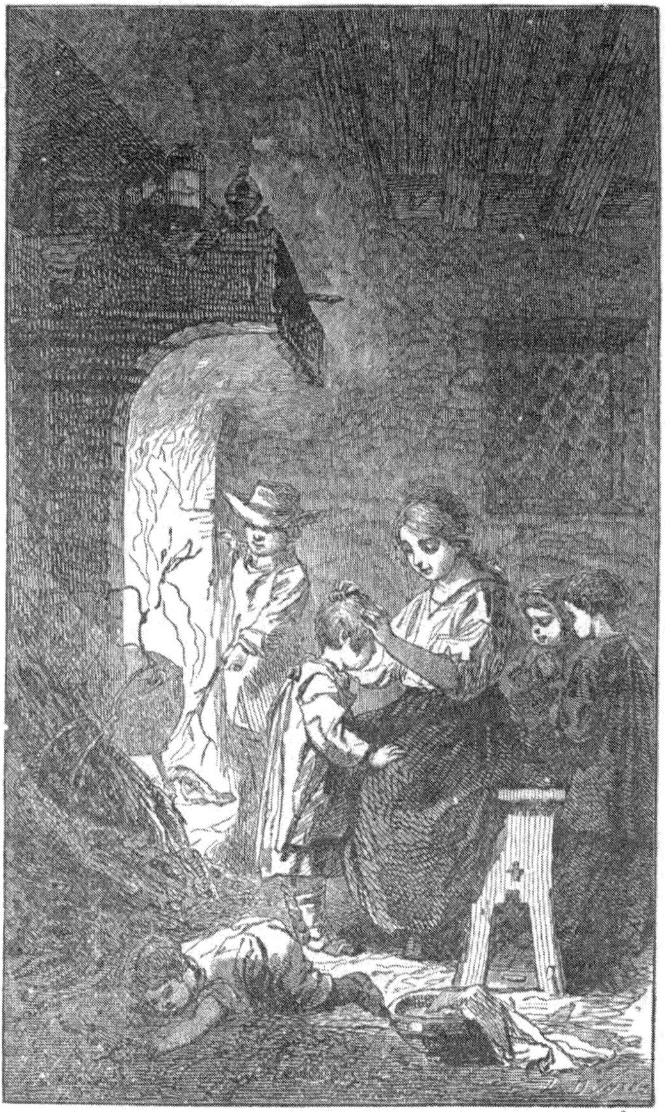

Voyez Louise dans sa
Look at Louisa in her

chaumière, elle habille ses
cottage, she is dressing her

petits frères et ses petites
little brothers and her little

sœurs ; elle les peigne et les
sisters ; she combs them and

débarbouille ; elle a une
washes their faces ; she has one

sœur et quatre frères.
sister and four brothers.

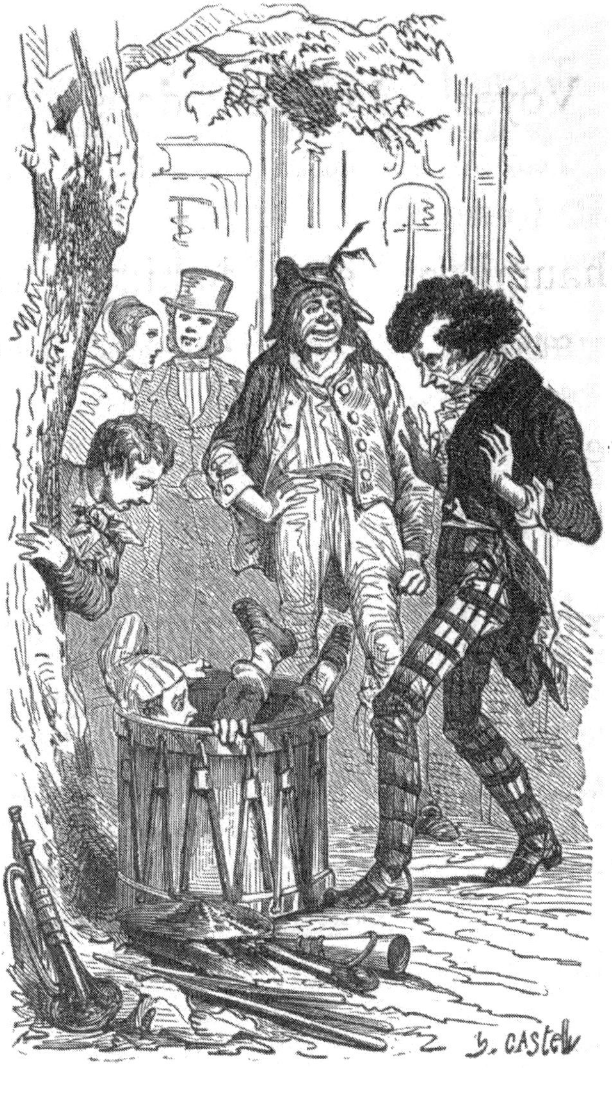
B. Castelli

Tiens ! qu'y a-t-il ? Arthur
Now then! what has happened? Arthur

est tombé ; il est tombé sur le
has fallen; he has fallen on the

tambour ; il a crevé le tam-
drum; he has burst the

bour et maintenant il est dans
drum, and now he is inside

le tambour. Arthur n'est pas
the drum. Arthur is not

content, et la personne à qui
pleased, and the person to whom

le tambour appartient n'est
the drum belongs is not

pas contente non plus.
pleased either.

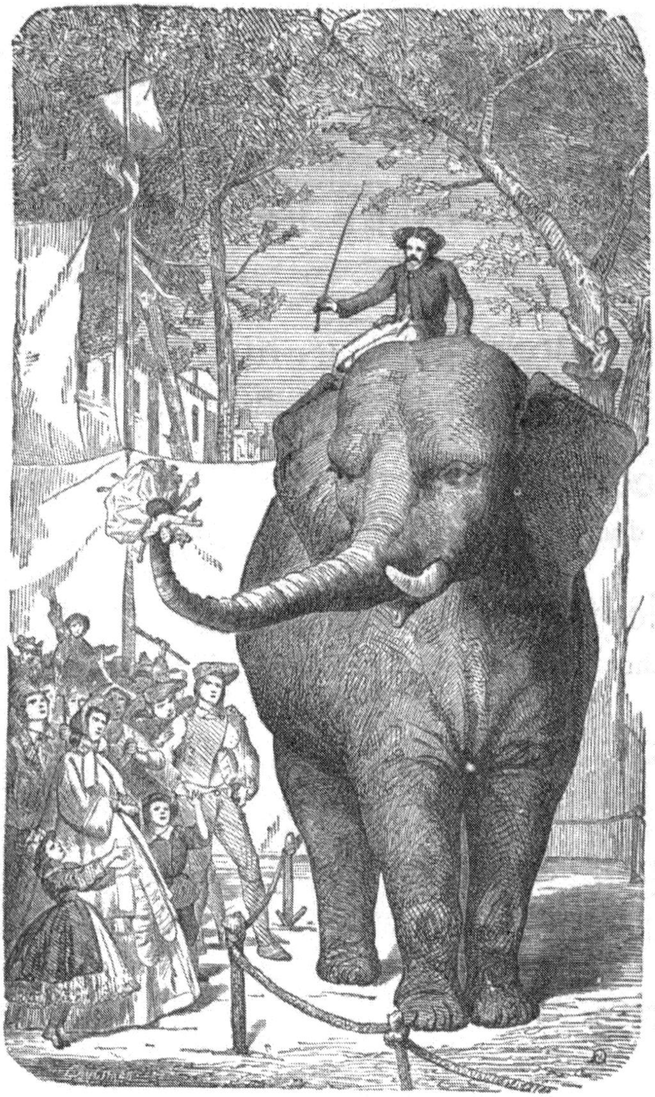

L'éléphant a pris la poupée
The elephant has taken Edith's doll
d'Edith avec sa trompe.
with his trunk.
J'espère qu'il ne lui fera pas
I hope that he will not
de mal. Edith a du chagrin.
hurt it. Edith is sorry.
Elle demande sa poupée.
She asks for her doll.
L'Eléphant n'est pas méchant,
The elephant is not cruel,
il lui rendra sa poupée, j'en
he will give her back her doll, I am
suis sûr.
sure.

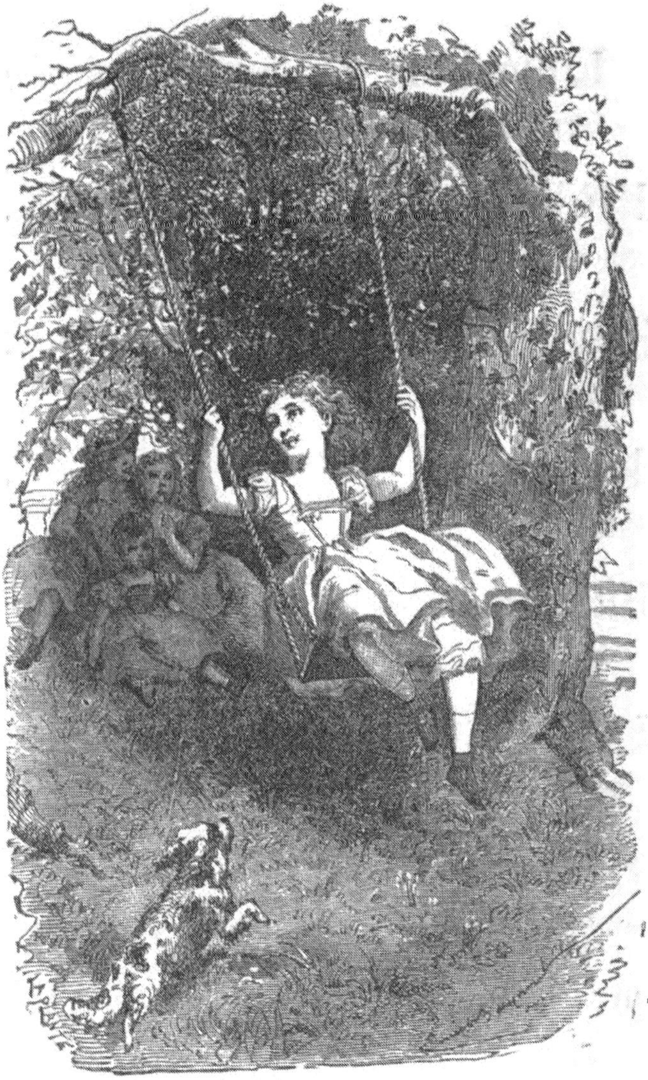

Emma a demandé à son
Emma has asked her

père de lui faire une balan-
father to make her a

çoire dans le jardin. Son
swing in the garden. Her

père, qui est très habile, lui en
father, who is very clever, has made

a fait une. Emma, enchantée,
her one. Emma, delighted,

se balance pendant que ses
swings whilst her

petites amies se reposent sur
little friends are resting on

l'herbe.
the grass.

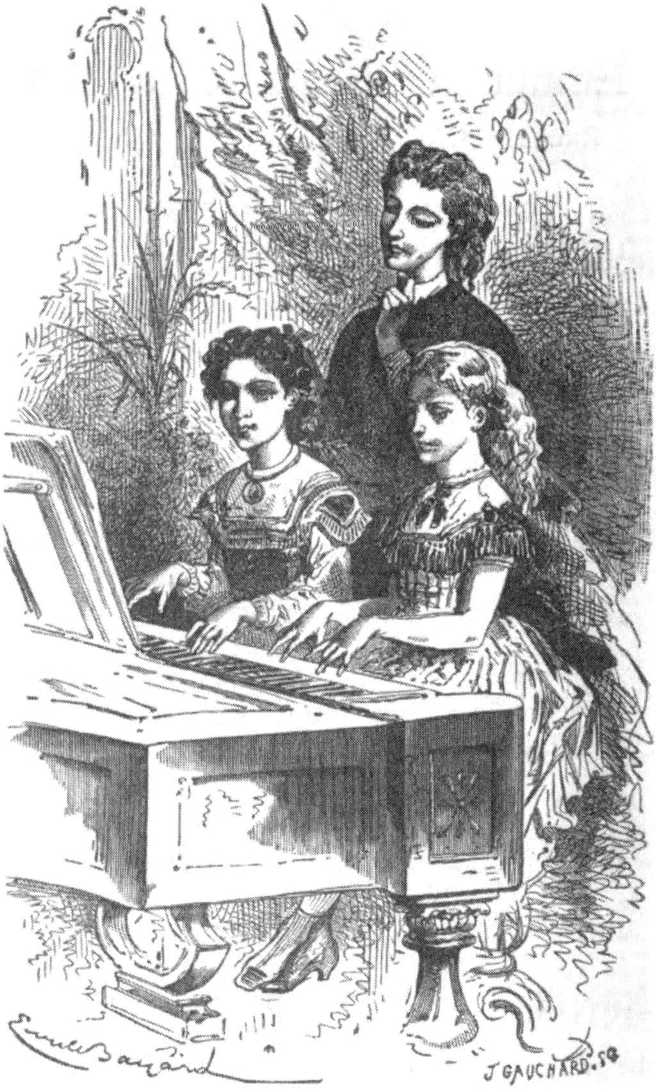
Emile Bayard
J GAUCHARD.SC

Julie et Rose sont très
Julia   and   Rosa   are   very

sages. Elles ont du goût
good.   They   have   a taste

pour la musique. Leur gou-
for   music.   Their   gover-

vernante est contente d'elles
ness   is   pleased   with them

car elles travaillent bien et
for   they   work   well   and

font des progrès. Elles jouent
make   progress.   They are playing

un morceau à quatre mains.
a duet.

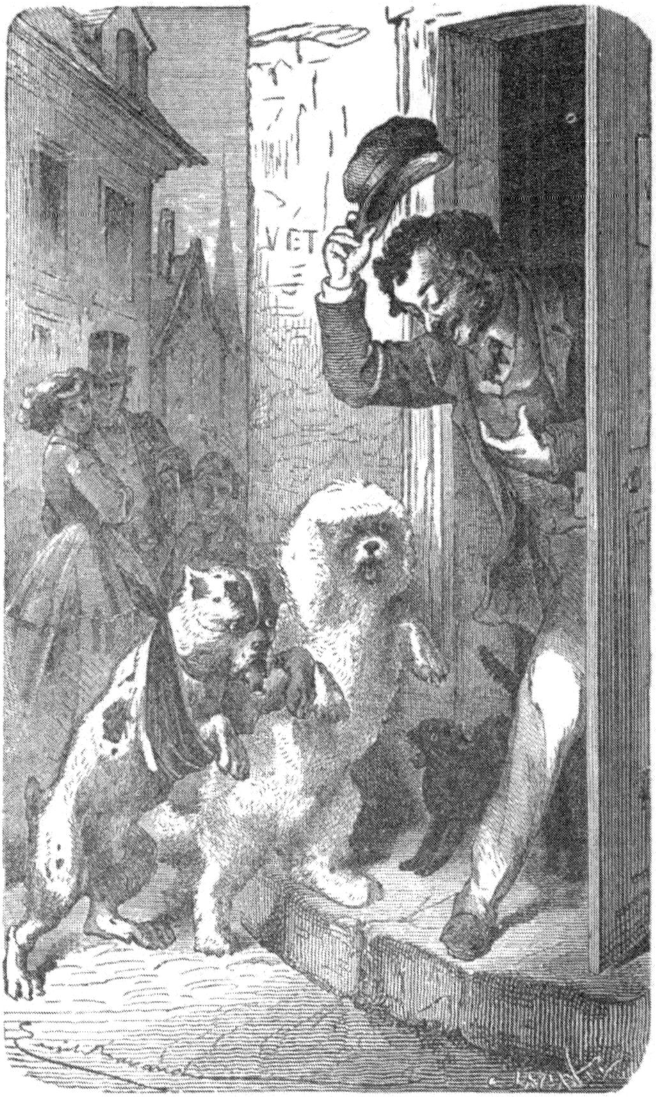

Le pauvre Hector s'est cas-
Poor　　　　Hector　　has broken

sé la patte ; son ami Wasp,
his paw ;　　　his　friend　Wasp,

qui se trouvait auprès de lui,
who　happened to be　　near him,

lui a mis la patte en écharpe
has put his paw　　in　a sling

et l'a conduit à l'hôpital des
and　has taken him　to　the hospital　for

chiens où le médecin en chef
dogs　where the　　chief doctor

les a reçus très poliment.
received them　very　politely.

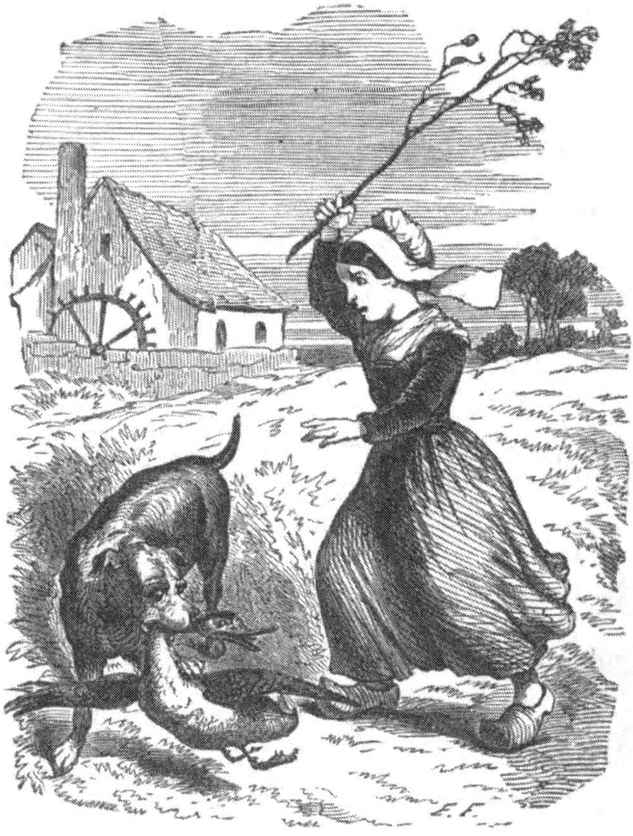

Tous les chiens ne sont pas
All dogs are not

aussi sages que Wasp; celui-
as good as Wasp; this

ci est un voleur; il a volé
one is a thief; he has stolen

une cane à cette pauvre fille.
a duck from this poor girl.

La cane crie très fort et la
The duck quacks very loud and the

fille frappe le chien avec son
girl is beating the dog with her

bâton.
stick.

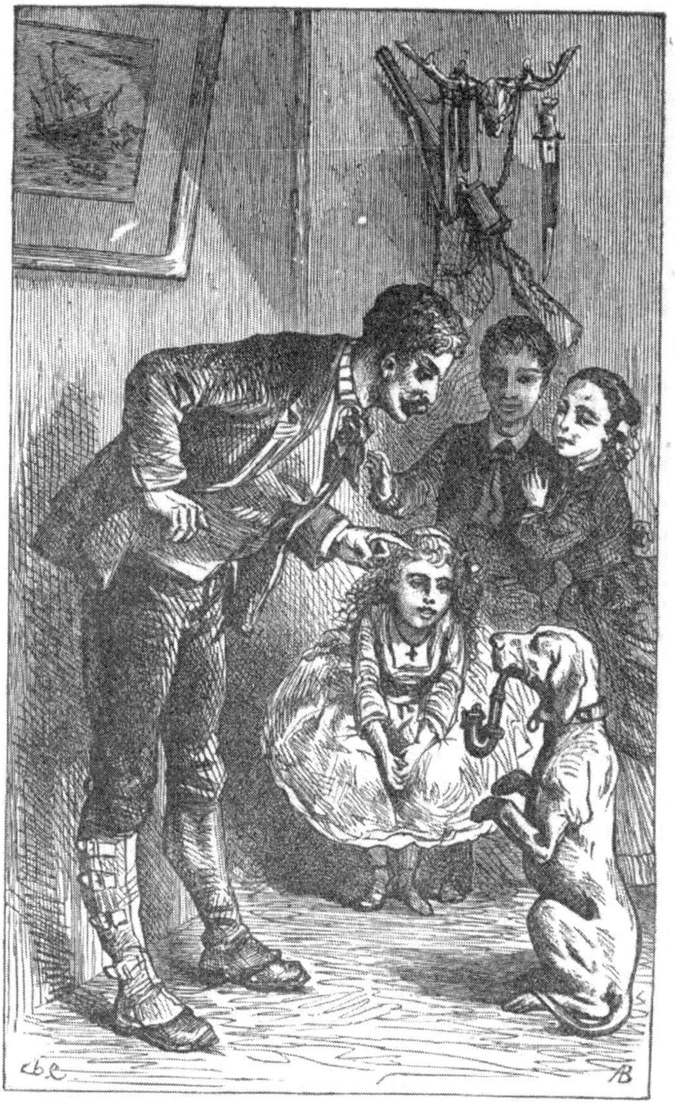

Ponto est très obéissant.
Ponto is very obedient.

Son maître lui a dit de faire
His master has told him

le beau, et Ponto fait le beau.
to beg and Ponto begs.

Il lui a dit de fumer sa pipe
He has told him to smoke his pipe

et il fume sa pipe; mais je
and he smokes his pipe; but I

crois qu'il n'aime pas beau-
do not think he enjoys that very

coup cela.
much.

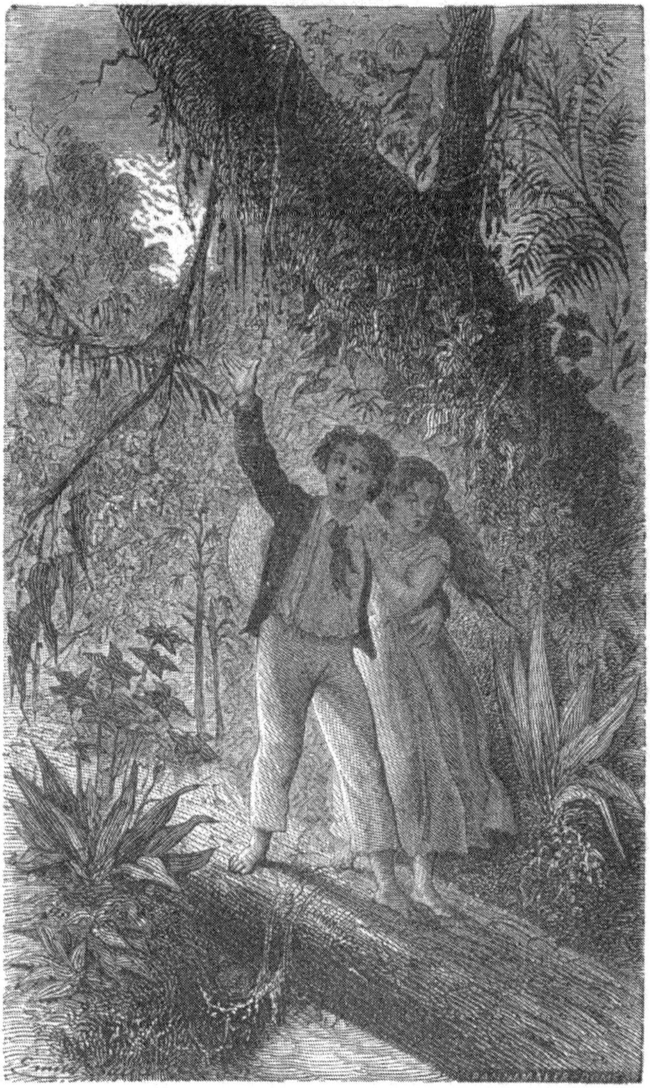

Paul et Virginie ont à tra-
Paul and Virginia have to

verser un torrent. Virginie a
cross a torrent. Virginia is

peur, mais Paul la soutient et
frightened, but Paul holds her up and

lui fait traverser le torrent sur
makes her cross the torrent on

un tronc d'arbre. Espérons
the trunk of a tree. Let us hope

qu'ils traverseront sans acci-
that they will cross without an acci-

dent.
dent.

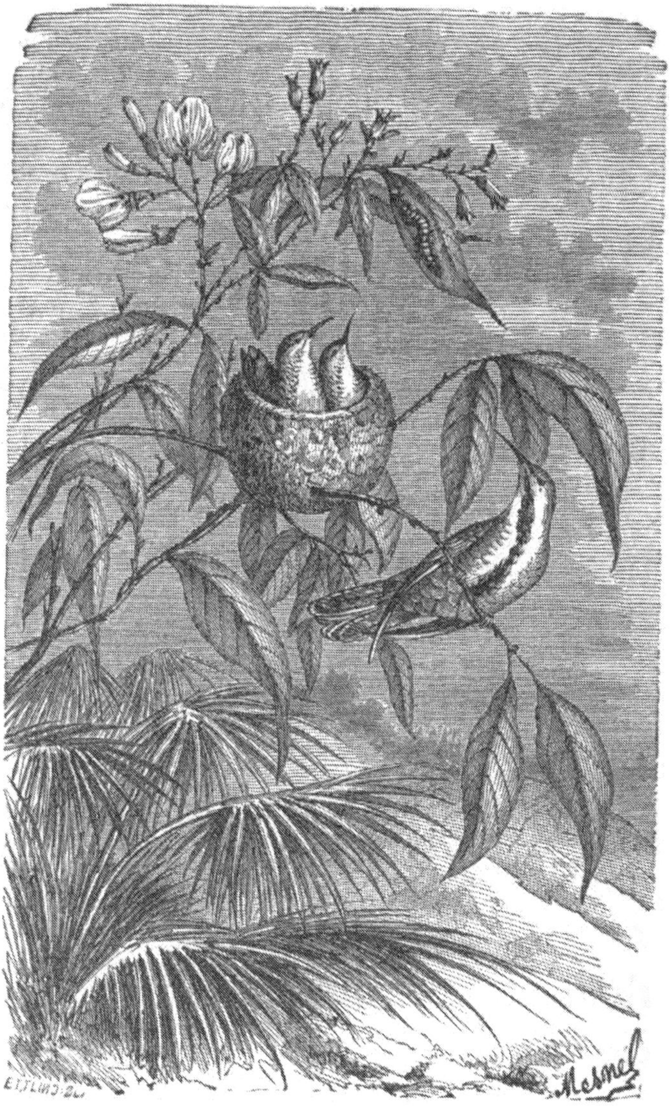

Voyez ce joli nid de coli-
See this pretty humming-bird's nest.

bris. Le colibri est un très
The humming-bird is a very

petit oiseau. Il a de très
small bird. It has some very

jolies plumes, un long bec
pretty feathers, a long, thin

mince, et il est très coura-
beak, and it is very brave.

geux.

Maintenant, mes chers
Now, my dear

enfants, je vais vous donner
children, I shall give you

quelques enfantines du bon
some nursery rhymes from the good

pays de France.
land of France.

CINQUIÈME PARTIE.
FIFTH PART.

FRENCH NURSERY RHYMES.

Dô Dô.
BYE-BYE.

Dô Dô.
Bye-Bye.

L'enfant dô,
Bye-Bye Baby.

L'enfant dormira tantôt.
Baby will sleep presently.

Noël.
CHRISTMAS.

Adieu Noël,
Good-bye Christmas,

Il est passé!
It is over!

Noël s'en va;
Christmas goes;

Il reviendra.
It will return.

Un, Deux, Trois.
ONE, TWO, THREE.

Moi,
I,

Toi
You

Et le Roi
And the King

Nous faisons trois.
We make three.

L'Araignée.
THE SPIDER.

Araignée le matin,
A spider in the morning

Chagrin,
Means sorrow,

A midi,
At noon

Plaisir;
Pleasure;

Le soir,
In the evening,

Espoir!
Hope!

Petit Bonhomme vit Encore!
THE LITTLE MAN IS ALIVE STILL!

1.—Je vous vends mon allumette,
    I   sell you   my little match,

Toute vivante, toute vivelette!
All   alive,   all   alive!

2.—Je vous prends votre allumette,
    I take your   little   match,

Toute vivante, toute vivelette!
All   alive,   all   alive!

N.B.—The player who passes the lighted bit of wood says No. 1; the one who takes it from him says No. 2.

Trop Serré.
TOO TIGHT.

Je n'peux pas danser,
  I   can't   dance,

Ma pantoufle est trop étroite;
My   slipper is too tight;

Je n'peux pas danser
  I   can't   dance

Parce que j'ai trop mal au pied!
Because my foot hurts me so!

Du Feu!
FIRE!

Chauffons! Chauffons!
Let us warm ourselves!

Ma commère Jeanneton,
Mother   Janet,

Prête-moi ton faucillon
Lend me your bill-hook

Pour couper une épinette
To   cut some wood

Pour chauffer ma p'tite fillette.
To   warm my little girl.

N.B.—Épinette means properly hemlock spruce.

Le Guet.
THE WATCH.

Guet! bon guet!
Watch! good watch!

Il a frappé douze heures;
It has struck   twelve;

Guet! bon guet!
Watch! good watch;

Dormez dans vos demeures.
Sleep in your houses.

La Fin du Conte.
THE END OF THE TALE.

J'ai passé par la porte Saint-Denis,
I went under the gate Saint-Denis,

J'ai marché sur la queue d'une souris,
I stepped on the tail of a mouse,

La souris a fait cri cri!
The mouse said queeck, queeck!

Et mon p'tit conte est fini.
And there's an end to my tale.

Trente, Vingt-huit et Trente et Un.
THIRTY, TWENTY-EIGHT AND THIRTY-ONE.

Trente jours ont Novembre,
Thirty days have November,

Avril, Juin et Septembre;
April, June and September;

De vingt-huit il en est un,
There is a month of twenty eight,

Les autres en ont trente et un.
The others have thirty one.

Ah! Quel Nez!
OH! WHAT A NOSE!

Ah! quel nez!
Oh! what a nose!

Ah! quel nez!
Oh! what a nose!

Ah! comme il est allongé!
Oh! how long it has got!

Tout le monde en est étonné.
Everybody is astonished at it.

Pantin.
DANCING-JACK.

Que Pantin serait content,
How pleased Dancing-Jack would be,

S'il avait l'heur de vous plaire!
If he had the luck of pleasing!

Que Pantin serait content,
How pleased Dancing-Jack would be,

S'il vous plaisait en dansant!
If he could please you by dancing!

Ne Prenez pas ma Place!
DON'T TAKE MY PLACE!

1.—C'est aujourd'hui la Saint-Hubert,
   It is   to-day   Saint-Hubert's day,

   Qui quitte sa place la perd.
   Who leaves his place loses it.

2.—C'est aujourd'hui la Saint-Laurent,
   It is   to-day   Saint-Laurence's day,

   Qui quitte sa place la reprend.
   Who leaves his place takes it back.

Les Doigts.
THE FINGERS.

1.—Celui-ci a été à la chasse,
   This little one went a-shooting,

2.—Celui-ci l'a tué,
   This little one killed the game,

3.—Celui-ci l'a plumé,
   This little one plucked it,

4.—Celui-ci l'a fait cuire
   This little one cooked it

5.—Et celui-ci l'a tout mangé.
   And this little one ate it all.

1. Le pouce, the thumb; 2. l'index, the fore-finger; 3. le majeur, the middle-finger; 4. l'annulaire, the ring-finger· 5. l'auriculaire, the little finger.

La Semaine.
THE WEEK.

—Bonjour, Monsieur Lundi.
Good day to you, Mr. Monday.

Comment va Monsieur Mardi ?
How is Mr. Tuesday ?

—Très bien, Monsieur Mercredi.
Very well, Mr. Wednesday.

—Je viens de la part de Monsieur Jeudi
I come from Mr. Thursday

Dire à Monsieur Vendredi
To tell Mr. Friday

Qu'il s'apprête Samedi
To get ready on Saturday

Pour aller à l'église Dimanche.
To go to church on Sunday.

Une, Deux, Trois.
ONE, TWO, THREE.

Une, deux, trois,
One, two, three,

J'irai dans le bois
I shall go into the wood

Quatre, cinq, six,
Four, five, six,

Cueillir des cerises,
To gather some cherries,

Sept, huit, neuf,
Seven, eight, nine,

Dans un panier neuf,
In a new basket,

Dix, onze, douze,
Ten, eleven, twelve,

Elles seront toutes rouges.
They will be quite red.

Les Trois Poules.
THE THREE HENS.

Quand trois poules vont aux champs,
When three hens go to the fields,

La premièr' march' par devant,
The first walks in front,

La second' suit la première,
The second follows the first,

La troisièm' march' la dernière.
The third comes last.

Quand trois poules vont aux champs,
When three hens go to the fields,

La premièr' march' par devant.
The first walks in front.

Ramasse une Épingle.
PICK UP A PIN.

Vois une épingle et ramasse-la,
See a pin and pick it up,

Tout le jour bonne chance auras;
All the day you'll have good luck;

Vois une épingle et laisse-la là,
See a pin and let it lay,

Et tu t'en repentiras.
Bad luck you'll have all day.*

* Literally "and you will repent it."

Le Premier Mot de L'Enfant.
THE CHILD'S FIRST WORD.

L'aurore vermeille
The rosy morn

Éveille
Awakes

L'enfant aux beaux yeux
The child with bright

Joyeux.
And pretty eyes.

Et son doux sourire
And its sweet smile

Expire
Ends

Dans ce mot charmant :
In this charming word :

Maman !
Mamma !

Le Petit Coq qui sort de l'Œuf.
THE LITTLE COCK COMING OUT OF THE EGG.

Tic, tac, toc,
Tick, tack, tock,

Quel est ce coup sec ?
What is this sharp knock ?

Ric, rac, roc,
Rick, rack, rock,

C'est d'un petit bec
It is a little beak

Cric, crac, croc,
Crick, crack, crock,

La coquille casse ;
The shell cracks ;

Fric, frac, froc,
Frick, frack, frock,

C'est l'ergot qui passe,
It is the spur coming out,

Clic, clac, cloc,
Click, clack, clock,

C'est le petit coq.
It is the little cock.

Petit Pied Rose.
LITTLE ROSY FOOT.

Petit pied, petit pied rose
Little foot, little rosy foot

De mon bien-aimé qui dort,
Of my beloved babe who sleeps,

Toi qui vacilles encor
You who still totter

Quand par terre je te pose ;
When touching the ground ;

Alors que tu marcheras
When you can walk

Petit pied, petit pied rose,
Little foot, little rosy foot,

Alors que tu marcheras
When you can walk

Qui sait où tu passeras !
Who knows where you will go !

L'Enfant Gâté.
THE SPOILED CHILD.

Enfant gâté
Spoiled child

Veux-tu du pâté ?
Will you have some pie ?

—Non, ma mère, il est trop salé.
No, mother, it is too salt.

—Veux-tu du rôti ?
Will you have some roast beef ?

—Non, ma mère, il est trop cuit.
No, mother, it's too much done.

—Veux-tu de la salade ?
Will you have some salad ?

—Non, ma mère, elle est trop fade.
No, mother, it is tasteless.

—Veux-tu du pain ?
Will you have some bread ?

—Non, ma mère, il ne vaut rien
No, mother, it isn't good.

—Enfant gâté,
Spoiled child,

Tu ne veux rien manger;
You will eat nothing;

Enfant gâté,
Spoiled child,

Tu seras fouetté !
You will get a flogging!

Le Mariage de la Bécasse et de la
THE WEDDING OF THE WOODCOCK AND THE
Perdrix.
PARTRIDGE.

La bécasse et la perdrix
The woodcock and the partridge

Vont se marier lundi ;
Are going to marry on Monday ;

Ils ont bien de monde assez,
They have quite enough guests,

Mais de pain il n'en ont point.
But they have no bread.

Par là passent deux pigeons
See yonder come two pigeons

Dans leur bec tiennent un pain rond ;
With a round loaf in their beaks ;

Ils ont bien de pain assez,
Now they have quite enough bread,

Mais de viande il n'en ont point.
But they have no meat.

Par là passent trois corbeaux
See yonder come three crows

Dans leur bec tiennent un gigot ;
With a leg of mutton in their beaks ;

Ils ont bien de viande assez,
Now they have enough meat

Mais de vin ils n'en ont point.
But they have no wine.

Par là passent six souris
See yonder come six mice

Sur leur queue tiennent un baril;
With a barrel on their tails;

Ils ont bien de vin assez,
Now they have quite enough wine,

Mais de musique n'en ont point.
But they have no music.

Par là passent trois gros rats
See yonder come three big rats

Tenant un violon sous leurs bras;
With a fiddle under their arms;

—Bonjour, bonjour, la compagnie,
Good-morning, good-morning all,

N'y a-t-il pas de chats ici ?
Are there no cats here ?

—Entrez, entrez, mes beaux messieurs,
Come in, come in, my fine sirs,

Le chat dort au coin du feu.
The cat's asleep by the fire.

Le chat s'étant éveillé
But the cat awoke

Mangea toute la société !
And ate up all the company!

Le Petit Oiseau.
THE LITTLE BIRD.

Enfin nous te tenons,
At last we have got you,

Petit, petit oiseau;
Little, little birdie;

Enfin nous te tenons
At last we have got you,

Et nous te garderons.
And we will keep you.

—Dieu m'a fait pour voler,
God made me to fly,

Gentils, gentils enfants,
Dear, dear children,

Dieu m'a fait pour voler,
God made me to fly,

Laissez-moi m'en aller
Let me fly away.

—Non, nous te donnerons,
No, we will give you,

Petit, petit oiseau,
Little, little birdie,

Non, nous te donnerons,
No, we will give you,

Biscuits, sucre, bonbons.
　Biscuits, sugar and sweets.

—Ce qui doit me nourrir,
　What is to feed me,

Gentils, gentils enfants,
　Dear, dear children,

Ce qui doit me nourrir,
　What is to feed me,

Aux champs seul peut venir.
　Grows only in the fields.

—Nous te gardons encor
　We keep for you besides,

Petit, petit oiseau,
　Little, little birdie,

Nous te gardons encor
　We keep for you besides

Une cage en fil d'or.
　A cage with gold wires.

—La plus belle maison,
　The finest house,

Gentils, gentils enfants,
　Dear, dear children,

La plus belle maison,
The   finest house,

Pour moi n'est que prison.
Is but a prison for me.

—Tu dis la vérité,
You have spoken the truth,

Petit, petit oiseau,
Little, little birdie,

Tu dis la vérité,
You have spoken the truth,

Reprends ta liberté.
Be free again.

Le Blé.
THE CORN.

Tica, tica, tac
Tick, tick, tack

Dans le moulin
In the mill

Le bon grain
The good corn

Devient belle farine.
Becomes fine flour.

Tica, tica, tac
Tick, tick, tack

Dans le moulin
In the mill

La meule écrase le grain.
The millstone crushes the corn.

Gué, gué, bons paysans,
Gay! gay! good peasants,

Le monde a faim, du courage!
The people are hungry, courage!

A l'ouvrage!
To work!

Gué, gué, bons paysans,
Gay, gay, good peasants,

Vivent les bœufs, la charrue et les champs!
Hurrah! for the oxen, the plough and the fields!

Ah! tu sortiras Biquette.
OH! COME OUT NANNY-GOAT.

Ah! tu sortiras biquette, biquette,
Oh! come out nanny-goat,

Ah! tu sortiras de ces choux-là!
Oh! come out of that cabbage field!

Il faut aller chercher le loup!
We must go and fetch the wolf!

Le loup n'veut pas manger biquette,
The wolf won't eat nanny-goat,

Biquett' n'veut pas sortir des choux.
Nanny-goat won't come out of the cabbage field.

Ah ! tu sortiras biquette, etc.
Oh ! come out nanny-goat, etc.

Il faut aller chercher le chien!
We must go and fetch the dog!

Le chien n'veut pas mordre le loup,
The dog won't bite the wolf,

Le loup n'veut pas manger biquette,
The wolf won't eat nanny-goat,

Biquett' n'veut pas sortir des choux.
Nanny-goat won't come out of the cabbage field.

Ah ! tu sortiras, etc., etc.
Oh ! come out, etc., etc.

Il faut aller chercher l'bâton !
We must go and fetch the stick !

L'bâton n'veut pas battre le chien,
The stick won't beat the dog,

Le chien n'veut pas mordre le loup,
The dog won't bite the wolf,

Le loup n'veut pas manger biquette,
The wolf won't eat nanny-goat,

Biquett' n'veut pas sortir des choux.
And nanny-goat won't come out of the cabbage field.

Ah! tu sortiras, etc., etc.
Oh! come out, etc., etc.

Il faut aller chercher l'fermier!
We must go and fetch the farmer!

L'fermier veut bien prend' le bâton,
The farmer will take the stick,

L'bâton veut bien battre le chien,
The stick will beat the dog,

Le chien veut bien mordre le loup,
The dog will bite the wolf,

Le loup veut bien manger biquette,
The wolf will eat nanny-goat,

Biquett' veut bien sortir des choux,
Nanny-goat will come out of the cabbage field.

Ah! tu sortiras, etc., etc.
Oh! come out, etc., etc.

La Chanson de la Laine.

THE SONG OF THE WOOL.

I.

La laine du mouton
The wool of the sheep

Demande à être tondu;
   Must be   sheared;

On la tond, on la tond,
  It is sheard, it is sheard,

La laine du mouton.
The wool of the sheep.

II.

La laine du mouton
The wool of the sheep

Demande à être lavée;
   Must be   washed;

On la lave, on la lave,
It is washed, it is washed,

La laine du mouton.
The wool of the sheep.

III.

La laine du mouton
The wool of the sheep

Demande à être séchée;
Must be dried;

On la sèche, on la sèche,
It is dried, it is dried,

La laine du mouton.
The wool of the sheep.

IV.

La laine du mouton
The wool of the sheep

Demande à être étirée;
Must be stretched;

On l'étire, on l'étire,
It is stretched, it is stretched,

La laine du mouton.
The wool of the sheep.

V.

La laine du mouton
The wool of the sheep

Demande à être cardée;
Must be combed;

On la carde, on la carde,
It is combed, it is combed,

La laine du mouton.
The wool of the sheep.

VI.

La laine du mouton
The wool of the sheep

Demande à être filée;
Must be spun;

On la file, on la file,
It is spun, it is spun,

La laine du mouton.
The wool of the sheep.

VII.

La laine du mouton
The wool of the sheep

Demande à être tordue;
Must be twisted;

On la tord, on la tord,
It is twisted, it is twisted,

La laine du mouton.
The wool of the sheep.

VIII.

La laine du mouton
The wool of the sheep

Demande à être tricotée;
Must be knitted;

On la tricote, on la tricote,
It is knitted, it is knitted,

La laine du mouton.
The wool of the sheep.

IX.

La laine du mouton
The wool of the sheep

Demande à être portée ;
Must be worn ;

On la porte, on la porte,
It is worn, it is worn,

La laine du mouton.
The wool of the sheep.

X.

La laine du mouton
The wool of the sheep

Demande à s'user ;
Must be worn out ;

On l'use, on l'use,
It is worn out, it is worn out.

La laine du mouton.
The wool of the sheep.

Les Noces du Roitelet
THE WREN'S WEDDING.

Aux noces du roitelet
At the wren's wedding

L'époux est tout petit.
The bridegroom is very small.

Il part en tournée
He goes his rounds

Pour faire les invitations.
To invite his friends.

Venez avec un petit présent chacun
Come with a little present each of you

Car hélas ! il n'est pas riche.
For alas !   he is not rich.

J'irai, dit la corneille,
I shall go, said the crow,

Et je porterai du pain.
And I shall bring some bread.

J'irai aussi, dit la pie,
I shall go too, said the magpie,

Et je porterai une pièce de viande.
And I shall bring a piece of meat.

J'irai aussi, dit le geai,
I shall go too, said the jackdaw,

Et je porterai un pot de vin.
And I shall bring a can of wine.

J'irai aussi, dit la bécasse,
I shall go too, said the woodcock,

Et je ferai le prêtre.
And I shall be the priest.

J'irai aussi, dit la bécassine,
I shall go too,   said the snipe,

Pour aider à sonner la cloche.
To help to ring the bell.

J'irai aussi, dit le coucou,
I shall go too, said the cuckoo,

Avec un tambour sur mon dos.
With a drum on my back.

J'irai aussi, dit le milau,
I shall go too, said the kite,

Et j'irai chercher de l'eau.
And I shall go and fetch the water.

J'irai aussi, dit le merle,
I shall go too, said the blackbird,

Et j'aurai de l'argent dans ma bourse.
And I shall have money in my purse.

J'irai aussi, dit le pivert,
I shall go too, said the woodpecker,

Et je porterai un faix de bois.
And I shall bring a load of wood.

J'irai aussi, dit l'alouette,
I shall go too, said the lark,

Et je chanterai au-dessus de la rivière.
And I shall sing above the river.

J'irai aussi, dit le chardonneret,
I shall go too, said the goldfinch,

Et je chanterai près de la porte.
And I shall sing near the door.

J'irai aussi, dit l'hirondelle,
I shall go too, said the swallow,

Et je chanterai sur le faîte.
And I shall sing on the roof.

J'irai aussi, dit l'épervier,
I shall go too, said the hawk,

Ensemble avec la tourterelle.
Together with the dove.

Moi aussi, dit la mésange,
I too, said the tomtit,

J'irai avec l'étourneau.
I shall go with the starling.

Moi aussi, dit le pinson,
I too, said the chaffinch,

J'irai avec la huppe.
I shall go with the hoopoe.

Tous les oiseaux s'y trouvèrent,
All the birds were there,

Il n'y en eut qu'un seul qui ne vint pas
One only did not come.

Aux noces du roitelet,
At the wren's wedding,

L'époux est tout petit.
The bridegroom is quite small.

NOTE.—Celui qui ne vint pas est l'aigle; l'aigle est jaloux du
The one who did not come was the eagle; the eagle is jealous of
roitelet. Roitelet en français veut dire "petit roi."
the wren. "Roitelet" (wren), in French means "little king."

La Petite Fourmi qui allait à Jérusalem.
THE LITTLE ANT WHO WENT TO JERUSALEM.

Il y avait une fois une petite fourmi qui
There was once a little ant that
allait à Jérusalem.
went to Jerusalem.

Elle rencontra la neige, et la neige gela
She met the snow, and the snow froze off
la patte à la petite fourmi qui allait à
the paw of the little ant that went to
Jérusalem.
Jerusalem.

O neige, que tu es forte, toi qui gèles
Oh! snow, how strong you are, you who freeze
la patte à la petite fourmi qui va à Jé-
off the paw of the little ant that goes to Jerusalem.
rusalem.

Et la neige répondit: Bien plus fort est
And the snow answered: Much stronger is
le soleil qui me fond.
the sun that melts me.

O soleil, que tu es fort, toi qui fonds la
Oh! sun, how strong you are, you who melt the

neige, qui gèle la patte à la petite fourmi
snow, that freezes off the paw of the little ant

qui va à Jérusalem.
that goes to Jerusalem.

Et le soleil répondit: Bien plus fort est
And the sun answered: Much stronger is

le nuage qui me voile.
the cloud that hides me.

O nuage, que tu es fort, toi qui voiles le
Oh! cloud, how strong you are, you who hide the

soleil, qui fond la neige, qui gèle la patte
sun, that melts the snow, that freezes off the paw

à la petite fourmi qui va à Jérusalem.
of the little ant that goes to Jerusalem.

Et le nuage répondit: Bien plus fort est
And the cloud answered: Much stronger is

le vent qui me chasse.
the wind that drives me away.

O vent, que tu es fort, toi qui chasses le
Oh! wind, how strong you are, you who drive away the

nuage, qui voile le soleil, qui fond la neige,
cloud   that hides the sun,   that melts the snow,

qui gèle la patte à la petite fourmi qui va
that freezes off the paw of the little   ant   that goes

à Jérusalem.
to Jerusalem.

 Et le vent répondit : Bien plus forte est
 And the wind answered : Much stronger is

la montagne qui m'arrête.
the mountain that stops me.

 O montagne, que tu es forte, toi qui arrêtes
 Oh ! mountain, how strong you are, you who stop

le vent, qui chasse le nuage, qui voile le
the wind, that drives away the cloud, that hides the

soleil, qui fond la neige, qui gèle la patte
sun, that melts the snow, that freezes off the paw

à la petite fourmi qui va à Jérusalem.
of the little ant that goes to Jerusalem.

 Et la montagne répondit : Bien plus forte
 And the mountain answered : Much stronger

est la souris qui me perce.
is the mouse that pierces me.

O souris, que tu es forte, toi qui perces
Oh! mouse, how strong you are, you who pierce

la montagne, qui arrête le vent, qui chasse
the mountain, that stops the wind, that drives away

le nuage, qui voile le soleil, qui fond la
the cloud, that hides the sun, that melts the

neige, qui gèle la patte à la petite fourmi
snow, that freezes off the paw of the little ant

qui va à Jérusalem.
that goes to Jerusalem.

Et la souris répondit : Bien plus fort
And the mouse answered: Much stronger

est le chat qui me mange.
is the cat that eats me.

O chat, que tu es fort, toi qui manges la
Oh! cat, how strong you are, you who eat the

souris, qui perce la montagne, qui arrête
mouse, that pierces the mountain, that stops

le vent, qui chasse le nuage, qui voile le
the wind, that drives away the cloud, that hides the

soleil, qui fond la neige, qui gèle la patte
sun, that melts the snow, that freezes off the paw

à la petite fourmi qui va à Jérusalem.
of the little ant that goes to Jerusalem.

Et le chat répondit : Bien plus fort est le
And the cat answered : Much stronger is the

chien qui m'effraie.
dog that frightens me.

O chien, que tu es fort, toi qui effraie le
Oh! dog, how strong you are, you who frighten the

chat, qui mange la souris, qui perce la
cat, that eats the mouse, that pierces the

montagne, qui arrête le vent, qui chasse
mountain, that stops the wind, that drives away

le nuage, qui voile le soleil, qui fond la
the cloud, that hides the sun, that melts the

neige, qui gèle la patte à la petite fourmi
snow, that freezes off the paw of the little ant

qui va à Jérusalem.
that goes to Jerusalem.

Et le chien répondit : Bien plus fort est
And the dog answered : Much stronger is

le bâton qui me frappe.
the stick that strikes me.

O bâton, que tu es fort, toi qui frappes
Oh! stick, how strong you are, you who strike

le chien, qui effraie le chat, qui mange la
the dog, that frightens the cat, that eats the

souris, qui perce la montagne, qui arrête
mouse, that pierces the mountain, that stops

le vent, qui chasse le nuage, qui voile le
the wind, that drives away the cloud, that hides the

soleil, qui fond la neige, qui gèle la patte
sun, that melts the snow, that freezes off the paw

à la petite fourmi qui va à Jérusalem.
of the little ant that goes to Jerusalem.

Et le bâton répondit: Bien plus fort est
And the stick answered: Much stronger is

le feu qui me brûle.
the fire that burns me.

O feu, que tu es fort, toi qui brûles le
Oh! fire, how strong you are, you who burn the

bâton, qui frappe le chien qui effraie le
stick, that strikes the dog, that frightens the

chat, qui mange la souris, qui perce la
cat, that eats the mouse, that pierces the

montagne, qui arrête le vent, qui chasse
mountain, that stops the wind, that drives away

le nuage, qui voile le soleil, qui fond la
the cloud, that hides the sun, that melts the

neige, qui gèle la patte à la petite fourmi
snow, that freezes off the paw of the little ant

qui va à Jérusalem.
that goes to Jerusalem.

Et le feu répondit: Bien plus forte est
And the fire answered: Much stronger is

l'eau qui m'éteint.
the water that quenches me.

O eau, que tu es forte, toi qui éteins
Oh! water, how strong you are, you who quench

le feu, qui brûle le bâton, qui frappe le
the fire, that burns the stick, that strikes the

chien, qui effraie le chat, qui mange la
dog, that frightens the cat, that eats the

souris, qui perce la montagne, qui arrête
mouse, that pierces the mountain, that stops

le vent, qui chasse le nuage, qui voile le
the wind, that drives away the cloud, that hides the

soleil, qui fond la neige, qui gèle la patte
sun, that melts the snow, that freezes off the paw

à la petite fourmi, qui va à Jérusalem.
of the little ant, that goes to Jerusalem.

Et l'eau répondit : Bien plus forte est
And the water answered: Much stronger is
la vache qui me boit.
the cow that drinks me.

O vache, que tu es forte, toi qui bois
Oh! cow, how strong you are, you who drink
l'eau, qui éteint le feu, qui brûle le bâton,
the water, that quenches the fire, that burns the stick,
qui frappe le chien, qui effraie le chat, qui
that strikes the dog, that frightens the cat, that
mange la souris, qui perce la montagne,
eats the mouse, that pierces the mountain,
qui arrête le vent, qui chasse le nuage,
that stops the wind, that drives away the cloud,
qui voile le soleil, qui fond la neige, qui
that hides the sun, that melts the snow, that
gèle la patte à la petite fourmi qui va à
freezes off the paw of the little ant that goes to
Jérusalem.
Jerusalem.

Et la vache répondit : Bien plus fort est
And the cow answered: Much stronger is
l'homme qui me tue.
the man that kills me.

O homme, que tu es fort, toi qui tues la
Oh! man, how strong you are, you who kill the
vache, qui boit l'eau, qui éteint le feu,
cow, that drinks the water, that quenches the fire,
qui brûle le bâton, qui frappe le chien, qui
that burns the stick, that strikes the dog, that
effraie le chat, qui mange la souris,
frightens the cat, that eats the mouse,
qui perce la montagne, qui arrête le vent,
that pierces the mountain, that stops the wind,
qui chasse le nuage, qui voile le soleil, qui
that drives away the cloud, that hides the sun, that
fond la neige, qui gèle la patte à la petite
melts the snow, that freezes off the paw of the little
fourmi qui va à Jérusalem.
ant that goes to Jerusalem.

Et l'homme répondit : Bien plus fort est
And the man answered: Much stronger still is
encore Dieu qui a créé l'homme, qui tue
God who created the man, that kills
la vache, qui boit l'eau, qui éteint le feu,
the cow, that drinks the water, that quenches the fire,

qui brûle le bâton, qui frappe le chien, qui
that burns the stick, that strikes the dog, that

effraie le chat, qui mange la souris,
frightens the cat, that eats the mouse,

qui perce la montagne, qui arrête le vent, qui
that pierces the mountain, that stops the wind, that

chasse le nuage, qui voile le soleil, qui fond
drives away the cloud, that hides the sun, that melts

la neige, qui gèle la patte à la petite fourmi
the snow, that freezes off the paw of the little ant

qui va à Jérusalem.
that goes to Jerusalem.

Exercices de Prononciation.
EXERCISES ON PRONUNCIATION.

Chat vit rôt,
Pussy saw the roast beef,

Rôt tenta chat ;
The roast beef tempted pussy;

Chat mit patte à rôt,
Pussy put her paw to the roast beef,

Rôt brûle patte à chat.
The roast beef burnt pussy's paw.

Riz tenta rat;
The rice tempted the rat;

Rat tenté tâta riz.
The tempted rat ate the rice.

Ton thé t'a-t-il ôté ta toux ?
Has your tea taken away your cough ?

Didon dina, dit-on, du dos d'un dodu dindon.
Dido dined, they say,   off a fat turkey's back.

Combien ces six saucissons-ci ?
How much are these six sausages ?

—Six sous ces six saucissons-ci.
These six sausages are six sous.

—Six sous ces six saucissons-ci !
Six sous these six sausages !

Ces six saucissons-ci sont si chers !
These six sausages are so dear !

Voici six chasseurs sachant chasser.
Here are six huntsmen who can hunt.

Quatre plats plats dans quatre plats creux,
Four flat dishes in four hollow dishes,

Quatre plats creux dans quatre plats plats.
Four hollow dishes in four flat dishes.

Celui-là n'est pas ivre
.He is   not   tipsy

Qui trois fois peut dire :
Who three times can   say :

Blanc, blond, bois ⎫
White,   fair,   wood ⎪
Blond, bois, blanc ⎬ barbe grise, bois.
Fair,   wood,   white ⎪ grey   beard, wood
Bois, blond, blanc ⎪
Wood,   fair,   white ⎭

Devinettes.
RIDDLES.

Je l'ai vu vif, je l'ai vu mort,
   I saw it alive, I saw it dead,

Je l'ai revu vif après sa mort.
   I saw it alive again after its death.

Une bougie allumée, éteinte, puis rallumée de nouveau.
   A lighted candle, extinguished,   and then lighted again.

Six pieds, quatre oreilles,
   Six feet,   four   ears,

Deux bouches, deux fronts,
   Two   mouths,   two foreheads,

Quelle bête est-ce donc ?
   What animal is that then ?

     Un cheval et son cavalier.
     A   horse and its   rider.

Petite robe blanche
Little white dress

Sans couture ni manche.
Without seam nor sleeve.

Un œuf.
An egg.

Dis-moi, de grâce, quelle est la chose
Tell me, pray, what thing it is

Qui nuit ni jour ne se repose ?
That rests neither day nor night ?

La rivière.
The river.

Madame Grand-Manteau
Mrs. Great-Cloak

Couvre tout, excepté l'eau.
Covers all things but water.

La neige.
The snow.

Qui me nomme me rompt
He who names me breaks me.

Le silence.
Silence.

HENRI BUÉ'S
New Conversational French Course.

THE
ILLUSTRATED FRENCH PRIMER;
OR THE
Child's First French Lessons.

EDITED BY

HENRI BUÉ, B. ès L.,

*French Master at Merchant Taylors' School, London;
Occasional Examiner H.M.C.S.C.*

The easiest Introduction to the Study of French, with numerous Wood Engravings.

**New Edition. 1 vol. small 8vo. cloth.
Price 1s. 6d.**

"In H. Bué's 'Illustrated French Primer' we have a capital little introduction to the mysteries of the French language intended for very young children, and really adapted to their comprehension. The pronunciation of the letters is first explained and exemplified, and then the young pupil is led on to mastery of words, simple sentences, and idiomatic phrases. There is no inculcation of formal rules; the eye, ear, and memory are alone appealed to, and by the proper use of this book, teachers will be able to lay an excellent foundation for the future more systematic study of French."
—*Scotsman.*

"There is scarcely a page without a cleverly-executed engraving, and a child could certainly learn French from no better devised or more interesting manual."—*Literary Churchman.*

HENRI BUÉ'S
New Conversational French Course

EARLY FRENCH LESSONS
BY
HENRI BUÉ, B. ès L.,
French Master at Merchant Taylors' School, London
Occasional Examiner H.M.C.S.C.

The compiler of this little book has had in view to teach the young beginner as many French words as possible in the least tedious manner. He has found by experience that what children dislike most to learn are lists of words, however useful and well chosen, and that they very soon get weary of disconnected sentences, but commit to memory most readily a short nursery rhyme, anecdote, or fable. Hence the selection he has made.

New Edition. 64 Pages. Cloth, Price 8d.

THE
FIRST FRENCH BOOK
GRAMMAR, CONVERSATION, AND TRANSLATION.

DRAWN UP FOR THE REQUIREMENTS OF THE FIRST YEAR,

AND ADOPTED BY THE SCHOOL BOARD FOR LONDON, AND BY THE MINISTER OF EDUCATION FOR CANADA.

With a Synopsis of the Grammatical Rules and two Complete Vocabularies

EDITED BY
HENRI BUÉ, B. ès L.,
*French Master at Merchant Taylors' School, London;
Occasional Examiner H.M.C.S.C.*

208 pages, Cloth. New Edition. Price 10d.

HENRI BUÉ'S

New Conversational French Course.

Opinions of the Press, Headmasters, and Teachers.

OPINIONS OF THE PRESS.

"This is a book, small as regards size and price, but containing in quantity at least matter which would furnish four far larger and more pretentious volumes. M. Bué's method and treatment are excellent; to any person unacquainted with French, but wishing to study that language, or to any teacher wishing to form classes for its study, we can cordially recommend his work. Books for use in school or class are often compiled by others than teachers, and the result is not always satisfactory. M. Bué is a teacher himself, and his lessons show that he understands the difficulties his brethren may labour under, and the best means by which they can be surmounted. We are glad to learn that the volume under notice has been adopted by the London School Board."—*The Irish Teachers' Journal*, Feb. 2nd, 1878.

"This little book is a model both of cheapness and of completeness. In 150 pages it gives beginners the principal rules of the French accidence, thus enabling them to practise conversation after a very few lessons. M. Bué commences by a list of easy and useful words to be learned by heart; the elementary grammar comes next, each chapter being followed by a vocabulary and two exercises. The reading lessons which terminate the volume are amusing anecdotes of graduated difficulties, and the vocabularies are so compiled as to preclude the necessity of a separate dictionary. The pupil has thus in a very small duodecimo all the help he requires towards a quick and easy mastery of the elements of the French language."—*School Board Chronicle*.

"M. Bué's First French Book is much to be commended. The lessons are very gradual, and the rules are explained with a simplicity that must greatly help both teacher and pupil. At the end of each lesson a short vocabulary, a model exercise, and a conversation are given. At the end of the verbs is a 'short chapter for the inquisitive,' which is well worth getting up, even by more advanced pupils. The chief merit of elementary books of this kind lies in their arrangement, and in this respect we have seen no better book than M. Bué's."—*School Guardian*, Nov. 10th, 1877.

"A handy little volume, which may serve with advantage as an introduction to the study of more elaborate works."—*The Pictorial World*, Oct. 13, 1877.

"This is one of the best first-books to French that has ever been published. The difficulties of the language are presented in a series of exercises and lessons, through which the student is led before he realises that he has really had genuine difficulties presented to him. The vocabularies contained in the book have been selected very skilfully. 'A short chapter for the inquisitive' is excellent. There is a French-English vocabulary containing nearly 1,500 words in most frequent use."—*The Weekly Times*, Oct. 14, 1877.

"This is a very excellent little work, and will be welcomed both in schools and for private teaching. It bears the impress of an experienced teacher; and is marked with great care in pointing out the peculiarities of the language in construction, idiom, and pronunciation. The printing also deserves a word of notice, the variations in termination, &c., to which it is desired to call attention, being given in excellent bold type—so that the utmost use is made of the eye—probably the most powerful of all senses in assisting the memory, especially in the case of young people. There is no doubt that it will quite fulfil the author's wish, modestly expressed in the preface, of becoming 'a useful and handy primer.' "—*The London and China Express*, Oct. 12, 1877.

"A great deal more of the information needed by a beginner than much larger works often contain, will be found in this little pocket grammar and exercise book. Only an experienced teacher could so well anticipate the preliminary difficulties and remove them from the path of a young linguist as M. Bué has done in his primer."—*Public Opinion*, Nov. 10, 1877.

OPINIONS CONCERNING
H. BUÉ'S New Conversational French Course.
(Continued.)

Her Majesty's inspectors have strongly recommended to us your new series of French books by M. Bué.
STRATHAVEN, N.B.

Our pupil teachers have been using the First Book with very satisfactory results.
NEWCASTLE-UPON-TYNE.

I am very pleased that their stirling merit is not only appreciated in England, but in America and Australia.
W. F.

I have no hesitation in saying, that the compactness, as well as the general arrangement of the work, make it the best work of the kind that has yet come under my notice.
DUNMURRY, *March 14th*, 1884. R. H. G.

Two admirable books.
ONE OF H.M. I. OF SCHOOLS.

My knowledge of their worth is formed upon the opinion of a friend, well versed in French. He says: they are admirable.
ONE OF H.M. I. OF SCHOOLS.

I have used M. Bué's First and Second Books now for some years for large classes of children and pupil teachers, and have found them answer admirably.
LEEDS AND DISTRICT PUPIL TEACHERS PRIZE ASSOCIATION.

I have used M. Bué's little French Book with junior pupils, and find them excellent.
KINGSTOWN, DUBLIN *October 25th*, 1884.

HENRI BUÉ'S
New Conversational French Course.

THE
SECOND FRENCH BOOK
GRAMMAR, CONVERSATION,
AND TRANSLATION.

Drawn up according to the requirements of the second year,

And adopted by the School Board for London, and by the Minister of Education for Canada.

With two Complete Vocabularies.

Edited by
HENRI BUÉ, B. ès L.
*French Master at Merchant Taylors' School, London;
Occasional Examiner H.M.C.S.C.*

1 vol. 208 pages. New Edition. Cloth, price 1s.

The Key to the First and Second Books and to the First Steps in French Idioms.
For Teachers only. 1 vol., 2s. 6d.

Easy French Dialogues (*In preparation*).

A Primer of French Composition (*In preparation*).

An Elementary Conversational French Reader (*In preparation*).

HENRI BUÉ'S
New Conversational French Course.

FIRST STEPS IN FRENCH IDIOMS.
CONTAINING
An Alphabetical List of Idioms, Explanatory Notes, and Examination Papers.
Edited by **HENRI BUÉ, B. ès L.**,
French Master at Merchant Taylors' School, London;
Occasional Examiner H.M.C.S.C.
1 vol., 192 pages, cloth.   Price 1s. 6d.

"The present work is designed as an introduction to the *Expressions Idiomatiques Comparées*, and will be found extremely useful for students who wish to become acquainted with colloquial French. The words are arranged in alphabetical order, and the principal idiomatic phrases in which they occur are given, together with an English version. Excellent notes illustrate the origin of the various locutions, and a selection of one thousand sentences serves the purpose of examination tests."—*School Board Chronicle*.

"One of the commendable characteristics of this little book is that it gives intelligible reasons for idiomatic peculiarities. Another feature which will be found to be a recommendation is the supply of the key-word, which is to be taken into account in rendering English sentences into French. In these two particulars it is the best guide we have met with, and we recommend it to learners as a book they will find pleasure as well as profit in mastering."—*The British Mail*.

"Everyone who has acquired any knowledge of French is ever ready to admit that, perfect as his accent and his knowledge of the *finesse* of the language may be, its idioms are never mastered but by those who have for years lived on the other side of the Channel, and not even by many of these, although after a long study and anxious desire to read, write, and speak French as well as they can their own mother tongue. M. Bué has indeed grappled, tooth and nail, with this difficulty, by giving as complete a method of instruction for the conquering of this difficulty that could possibly be prepared. So perfect is the grasp of his subject, that he will have the blessings of thousands for having enabled them to overcome an obstacle that has hitherto been deemed and pronounced to be insuperable."—*Bell's Weekly Messenger*.

HENRI BUÉ'S
New Conversational French Course.

THE
NEW CONVERSATIONAL
First French Reader.

A collection of interesting narratives, adapted for use in Schools, with a list of the difficult words to be learned by heart, Conversation, Examination Questions, and a complete French-English Vocabulary.

EDITED BY

HENRI BUÉ, B. ès. L.,

French Master at Merchant Taylors' School, London;
Occasional Examiner H.M.C.S.C.

224 pages, cloth. Price 10d.

The above small volume will prove to be one of the most useful readers for beginners. The stories are chosen from favorite subjects. Each story is followed by a Conversation and some Examination Questions relating to the story.

The "Conversations" are intended as a guide for the pupil; they will show him how to avoid the abrupt "oui" and "non," and how to frame sentences in answer to his master's questions.

The master can, of course, vary his questions to any extent.

It is necessary to draw the pupil's attention to the more difficult words which occur in the piece he is translating, in order that he may know their meaning again when he meets with them elsewhere. The List of Words placed at the beginning of the book may be used in various ways for that purpose.

"The idea which has suggested the 'New Conversational First French Reader is excellent, and M. Bué has realised it with the greatest success. The pieces selected for translation are carefully graduated in point of difficulty, and the conversations which follow each extract are useful both with the view of immediate application and as models for other exercises of the same kind. The examination questions leave nothing to be desired, and the concluding vocabulary is very complete."

Harrow. GUSTAVE MASSON.

The idea is well carried out, and M. Bué displays a practical knowledge of the wants of English boys studying the language.—*Daily Chronicle.*

Ouvrages reçus en Dépôt.
Le Théâtre Français du XIX° Siècle.
Price per Volume, 9d.; in cloth, 1s.

CONTENTS.

(The Editors' Names are placed in Parenthesis.)

1. Hugo, *Hernani* (Gustave Masson).
2. Scribe, *Le Verre d'Eau* (Jules Bué).
3. Delavigne, *Les Enfants d'Edouard* (Francis Tarver).
4. Bouilly, *l'Abbé de l'Epée* (V. Kastner).
5. Mélesville et Duveyrier, *Michel Perrin* (Gustave Masson).
6. Sandeau, *Mademoiselle de la Seiglière* (H. J. V. de Candole.
7. Scribe, *Le Diplomate* A. Ragon).
8. Dumas, *Les Demoiselles de Saint-Cyr* (Francis Tarver).
9. Lebrun, *Marie Stuart* (H. Lallemand).
10. Labiche et Jolly, *La Grammaire* (G. Petilleau).
11. Girardin (Mme. de), *La Joie fait Peur* (Gérard).
12. Scribe, *Valérie* (A. Roulier).
13. Coppée, *Le Luthier de Crémone* (A. Mariette).
14. Coppée, *Le Trésor* (A. Mariette).
15. De Banville (Th.), *Gringoire* (Henri Bué).
16. Scribe et Legouvé, *Adrienne Lecouvreur* (A. Dupuis).
17. Labiche et Martin, *Voyage de M. Perrichon* (G. Petilleau).
18. Delavigne, *Louis XI.* (Francis Tarver).
19. Moinaux, *Les deux Sourds* (Blouët).
20. Scribe et Legouvé *Bataille de Dames* (E. Janau).

XAVIER DE MAISTRE,
La jeune Sibérienne; Le Lépreux de la Cité d'Aoste.
With a biographical sketch of the author, and grammatical and explanatory notes suitable for students preparing for examination. By V. KASTNER, M.A., Officier d'Académie. French Lecturer in Victoria University, Manchester.

1 vol. 144 pages.   *Cloth, price 1s. 6d.*

MADAME E. DE PRESSENSÉ.
Rosa.
With explanatory notes by G. MASSON, B.A., Officier d'Académie; late Assistant Master and Librarian, Harrow School.

1 vol. 299 pages.   *Cloth, price 2s.*

The difficulty of finding in the French language a really unexceptionable children's book is still often remarked; but Madame de Pressensé has, we believe, solved the problem. "ROSA" is a gem of its kind, and it is not too much to say that it would be impossible to select a volume combining a healthier religious and unsectarian tone with greater literary merit.

SOUVESTRE, E.
Le Philosophe sous les Toits,
JOURNAL D'UN HOMME HEUREUX.

With explanatory notes by JULES BUÉ, Hon. M.A. Oxford; Taylorian Teacher of French, Oxford; Examiner in the Oxford Local Examinations from 1858, etc.

1 vol. 232 pages.   *Cloth, price 1s. 6d.*

Ling's System — Swedish Gymnastics
Part I.—A Manual of Free Standing Movements.
For the use of Schools without apparatus. Compiled and arranged by J. D. Haasum, Captain 2nd Swedish Life Guards; Assistant Instructor, Royal Gymnastic Institute. With Illustrations. 1 vol., small 4to, cloth, price 1s. 6d.

Adopted by the School Board for London.

After having gone through a course of gymnastic instruction, founded on Ling's System, with the London School Board masters, and noted the interest exhibited for the work by the majority of those who attended my classes, as well as that shown by many Members of the Board, I have, encouraged and aided by Mr. T. Nordenfelt, decided to publish the following Tables, trusting they may be accepted in their book-form as a guide and help to all who intend promoting in this country the Swedish System of Physical Education, or adopting that method of body-culture for the benefit of those placed in their charge.

This little Manual consists of seven Tables, containing Free Standing Movements only, being designed for schools without apparatus. A series of Tabulated Exercises for schools possessing apparatus will shortly follow.

J. D H.

THE NEW GERMAN SERIES.

THE attention of the Heads of Colleges and Schools is respectfully directed to this New Series of German School Books, which has been projected with a view to supply a long-felt want, viz., thoroughly reliable Text-Books edited by German Scholars of the highest reputation, and at a price which will bring them within the reach of all. The series will comprise:—

VOL. I.
The German Primer.
Illustrated. Being the easiest Introduction to the study of German for all Beginners. Price 1s.

VOL. II.
The Children's Own German Book.
A selection of Amusing and Instructive Stories in Prose for Beginners. Edited by A. L. MEISSNER, M.A., Ph.D., D. Lit., Librarian and Professor of Modern Languages in Queen's College, Belfast. Small post 8vo. cloth, 1s. 6d.

VOL. III.
The First German Reader.
A Selection of Episodes from German History, &c. Edited by Dr. A. L. MEISSNER. Small post 8vo. cloth, 1s. 6d.

VOL. IV
Pictures of German Life.
A Select Number of Stories from Modern Authors. Edited by Dr. A. L. MEISSNER. Small post 8vo. cloth, 1s. 6d.

BUCHHEIM'S DEUTSCHE PROSA.
Two Volumes, sold separately, viz:—

VOL. V.
Schiller's Prosa.
Containing Selections from the Prose Works of Schiller with Notes for English Students. By Dr. BUCHHEIM, Professor of the German Language and Literature, King's College, London. Small post 8vo. cloth, 2s. 6d.

VOL. VI.
Goethe's Prosa.
Containing Selections from the Prose Works of Goethe, with Notes for English Students. By Dr. BUCHHEIM. Small post 8vo. cloth, 2s. 6d.

THE NEW GERMAN SERIES.—*Continued.*

Practical Lessons in German Conversation.

A Companion to all German Grammars, and an indispensable Manual for Candidates for the Civil and Military Services, and for Candidates for the Commercial Certificate of the Oxford and Cambridge Joint Board. By A. L. MEISSNER, M.A., Ph.D., D.Lit. 1 vol., cloth, 2s. 6d.

Bué's Class-Book of Comparative Idioms.

German Part. Edited by Professor R. LENNHEIM, late German Master to H.R.H. the Prince Imperial; and Dr. Th. WEHE, Principal German Master in Dulwich College, and late Lecturer of German at King's College. Cloth, price 2s.

Richard & Kaub's New English and German Dialogues.

New Edition, Revised and Corrected. With a Comparative Table of the new German Moneys, Weights, and Measures. Cloth, 32mo, price 1s. 6d. *Adopted by the School Board for London.*

Richard & Kaub's New English and German Word Book.

Cloth, 32mo, 80 pages, price 6d.

The German Newspaper Reading Book.

Containing Extracts from Forty Newspapers (revised according to the New Rules of German Orthography); Questions on Grammar and Philology based upon the Text; Classified Questions compiled from Papers set for the various Public Examinations; and a complete Summary of the changes recently introduced into German Orthography by the German Minister of Education.

Compiled and Edited by W. T. JEFFCOTT (Univ. Lond.), Vice-Principal of the High School, Margate; and G. J. TOSSEL (Univ. Lond.), Modern Language Master in the High School, Margate. 1 vol. small 8vo. Cloth, price 3s.

THE FIRST GERMAN BOOK.

GRAMMAR, CONVERSATION, AND TRANSLATION.
With a List of Useful Words to be committed to memory, and Two Vocabularies. By the Reverend A. L. BECKER. New Edition. Cloth, 196 pages, Price, 1s.

One Hundred Supplementary Exercises. Cloth, 1s.

Key for the two Parts (for Teachers only). Cloth, 2s. 6d.

OPINIONS OF THE PRESS.

"'The First German Book' seems to combine simplicity with clearness, in an admirable degree."—*Daily Chronicle*, October 9, 1880.

"Mr. Becker is good on separable and inseparable prefixes; and we are glad that he gives a long vocabulary of words to be learnt by heart (which, by the way, he prints in English as well as in German characters). The best German scholar we ever knew had laid his foundation by regularly learning sixty or eighty words a day.'—*The Graphic*.

"This neat little volume is strictly confined to teaching the elements of the German Language, and will prove useful alike to pupils in middle-class schools and to the self-student, who will value it as a useful and acceptable pocket companion. The various lessons appear to have been prepared with as much simplicity as possible, the aim of the author being to ensure the success of the learner by easy and agreeable stages."
—*The Exeter and Plymouth Gazette*.

"It is not often that so perfectly satisfactory a first book as this comes in our way. Though it is strictly confined to the essential elements of the language, these are so clearly stated and so admirably arranged that, provided the lessons are, as the author requires, 'thoroughly mastered,' a good practical knowledge may be acquired. The classification of the nouns and verbs is at once theoretically correct and practically easy. The brief chapter explaining the philology of German and English, and that on the interchange of letters in the two languages, will be found interesting and useful. This neat little volume is printed in clear, bold type, and may be had for the moderate price of One Shilling."—*The Athenæum*, October 9, 1880.

From the Reverend C. S. BERE, M.A. (Oxford).

"The book is admirably constructed. It is gradual and simple, and does not overwhelm the young student, at the outset of his study, with the many variations and exceptions with which each step is beset, but most of which need not be learnt till a fair acquaintance with a language has been attained. . . . The sentences for translation in this book are bright, natural, and not too numerous. . . . The short conversations (sometimes varied by the introduction of proverbs and familiar sayings) are also in natural language. They are such as are likely to take place, and not imaginary ones, which no one ever dreamt of using.

"A good *Vocabulary* is added, and the book itself is very handy and easily used. Altogether we do not know a more attractive book for the study of a language, difficult indeed of mastery, but inexhaustible in its treasures."—*The Blundellian*, October, 1880.

THE PUBLIC SCHOOL
GERMAN GRAMMAR,

With Exercises for Translation, Composition and Conversation.

By A. L. MEISSNER, M.A., Ph.D., D.Lit.,

Librarian and Professor of Modern Languages in Queen's College, Belfast.

Mitglied der Gesellschaft für das Studium der neueren Sprachen zu Berlin.

Vol. small 8vo. New Edition. 384 pages, cloth. Price 3s. 6d.

The **KEY** to the same (for teachers only), 3s.

German Authors.

With Grammatical and Explanatory Notes for English Schools. Price per volume 9d.

CONTENTS.

(The Editors' Names are placed in parenthesis.)

1. KOTZEBUE, "Der gerade Weg der beste." Lustspiel in einem Aufzuge. (A. C. CLAPIN.)
2. SCHILLER, "Der Parasit." (A. C. CLAPIN.)
3. KOTZEBUE, "Die deutschen Kleinstädter.' (E. L. NAFTEL.)
4. WICHERT, "Das eiserne Kreuz." (OTTO DELFS.)
5. SCHILLER, "Wilhelm Tell. (E. L. NAFTEL.)
6. GOETHE, "Hermann und Dorothea." (A. C. CLAPIN.)
7. R. BENEDIX, "Doktor Wespe." (E. L. NAFTEL.)

"The plays are prettily got up in paper covers, and will be an acquisition to students."—*Colliery Guardian*, Dec. 12, 1884.

"These are admirable little German lesson books, part of a series published by this eminent firm. The names of these gentlemen are a sufficient guarantee that the editing of these little primers has been skilfully and conscientiously done, and we have not the least doubt but that they will be found of great value to students of this important and fascinating language."—*Guernsey Star*.

11 Aug '38

Due 12 Feb '42   MAR 3 1969

DUE 2 Aug '48

DUE 6 Jan 50

DUE 20 Jan '50   FEB 1971

DUE Oct 21 '54

DUE 1 FEB '57
SUBJECT TO
RECALL

DEC 17 '57

DEC 1 1958

DEC 4 1961

MAY 3 0 1962

JUL 2 2 1963

Due 15 Dec 1966
Subject to
Recall